AF679480

Fundamentals of Information Technology:

A Comprehensive Guide

By Sha Md Farid

Dedication Page

This book is dedicated to every learner who wishes to understand Information Technology — not through complicated terminology or abstract theories, but through clear, practical, and accessible guidance. May these pages empower you to learn with confidence, curiosity, and purpose. To the students beginning their journey, the beginners striving to build a solid foundation, and the professionals who continue to expand their knowledge — may this book serve as a reliable companion, supporting your growth at every stage. It is also dedicated to all who believe in the transformative power of technology — to simplify life, connect people, and create a smarter, more compassionate world. And finally, to you, the reader — thank you for trusting this book to be part of your journey. Every question you ask, every challenge you overcome, and every skill you master is a step toward lifelong learning and meaningful expertise.

Preface Page

In today's interconnected world, Information Technology (IT) forms the heartbeat of modern society. From the smallest mobile device to vast global networks, technology defines how we work, communicate, and shape our future. This book was created with a single goal—to make IT simple, practical, and understandable for everyone. Whether you are a complete beginner or someone looking to strengthen your skills, this book takes you on a gradual journey from the basics to the essential concepts that power today's digital world. Each chapter has been written in clear, accessible language, supported by real-life examples and practical exercises. You will not only learn about technology but also experience how it works and why it matters. By the end of this book, you will have built a strong foundation in key areas of Information Technology, including:

- How computers and digital devices function
- The role of operating systems and application software
- Networking fundamentals and how the Internet works
- Core concepts of cybersecurity and safe digital practices
- Introduction to databases, programming, and cloud computing
- Insights into emerging fields such as Artificial Intelligence (AI) and the Internet of Things (IoT)
- Guidance on certifications, career paths, and opportunities in the IT industry

Unlike many technical guides, this book is not meant to overwhelm—but to empower. It bridges the gap between theory and real-world application, showing that IT is not only for experts, but for everyone willing to learn. Whether you are a student taking your first step into technology, a professional exploring new skills, or simply an enthusiastic learner seeking to understand the digital world—this book is for you.

Legal Disclaimer Page

This book is provided for educational purposes only. The author and publisher have made every effort to ensure the accuracy and reliability of the information contained herein. However: The material is provided "as is" without warranties of any kind, either express or implied. The author and publisher shall not be held liable for any errors, omissions, or damages arising from the use of this book. Technology evolves rapidly; readers are encouraged to verify information with up-to-date, authoritative sources.

Academic Integrity & Copyright Notice

This book is an original work created for the purpose of learning and instruction. The following applies:

1. Academic Integrity – The content is intended as a general educational reference. Readers are responsible for ensuring that their use of this material complies with their institution's academic integrity policies. The author is not liable for any misuse of the content for academic dishonesty, plagiarism, or other violations.

2. Unintentional Similarity Disclaimer – While every effort has been made to avoid plagiarism, any unintentional similarities with existing works are purely coincidental. The author does not claim ownership of external sources, trademarks, or referenced technologies.

3. Copyright – No part of this book may be reproduced, stored, or transmitted in any form or by any means (electronic, mechanical, photocopying, recording, or otherwise) without prior written permission of the author, except in the case of brief quotations for review, research, or educational purposes under fair use provisions.

Table of Contents

Chapter 1: Introduction to IT 1
1.1 What is IT? 2
1.2 Importance of IT in Daily Life 2
1.3. Evolution of Information Technology 2
1.4 Types of IT 4
1.5 IT Roles in Society 6
1.6 Practice Test 8
Chapter 2: Understanding Computer Hardware 11
2.1 Components of a Computer System 12
2.2 Input Devices 13
2.3 Output Devices 13
2.4 Storage Devices 14
2.5 Expansion Cards and Cooling Systems 14
2.6 Practice Test 15
Chapter 3: Software and Operating Systems 18
3.1 System Software 19
3.2 Application Software 20
3.3 Operating Systems 20
3.4 Mobile Apps and Web Apps 21
3.5 Software Installation and Updates 21
3.6 Practice Test 22
Chapter 4: Networking Fundamentals 26
4.1 Types of Networks 27
4.2 Internet Basics 28
4.3 Networking Devices 28
4.4. Wireless Technologies 30
4.5 Network Topologies 31

4.6 Practice Test 32

Chapter 5: The Internet 35

5.1. Understanding the Internet 36

5.2. IP Addresses, Domain Names, and DNS 36

5.3. How the Internet Connects the World 37

5.4. The Importance of the Internet in Modern Society 38

5.5 Practice Test 39

Chapter 6: Working with Data and Databases 42

6.1 Data, Information and Knowledge 43

6.2 Structured, Unstructured, and Semi-Structured Data 43

6.3 Relational Databases (SQL) 44

6.4 NoSQL Databases 44

6.5 Data Storage Formats 45

6.6 Practice Test 46

Chapter 7: Cybersecurity Essentials 50

7.1 Cyber Threats 51

7.2 Cybersecurity Principles 52

7.3 Firewalls and Antivirus Software 52

7.4 Encryption and VPNs 53

7.5 Social Engineering and Phishing Awareness 53

7.6 Practice Test 54

Chapter 8: IT Support and Troubleshooting 58

8.1 Common Hardware Issues 59

8.2 Common Software Issues 60

8.3 Troubleshooting Methodology 61

8.4 IT Support Tools 62

8.5 Preventive Maintenance and Best Practices 62

8.6 Practice Test 63

Chapter 9: Programming Fundamentals 66

9.1. What is Programming? 67

9.2. Algorithms and Flowcharts 67

9.3. Understanding Programming Languages 67
9.4. How and Where Programming Languages Are Used 68
9.5. Basic Debugging Techniques 69
9.6 Practice Test 70
Chapter 10: Web Technologies 73
10.1. HTML, CSS, and JavaScript Basics 74
10.2. Frontend vs Backend 74
10.3. Web Servers and Hosting 74
10.4. Responsive Web Design 75
10.5. Content Management Systems (CMS) 75
10.6 Practice Test 76
Chapter 11: Mobile and Smart Technologies 79
11.1 Smartphones and Tablets 80
11.2 IoT Devices and Wearable Technology 80
11.3 Embedded System 80
11.4 Mobile Application Ecosystems 81
11.5 Device Communication 81
11.6 Practice Test 82
Chapter 12: Virtualization and Cloud Services 85
12.1 Virtual Machines and Hypervisors 86
12.2 Benefits of Virtualization 86
12.3 Cloud Storage and Local Storage 86
12.4 Hybrid and Multi-Cloud Strategies 87
12.5 Docker and Containerization 87
12. 6 Practice Test 88
Chapter 13: Emerging Technologies 91
13.1 Artificial Intelligence and Machine Learning 92
13.2 Blockchain and Cryptocurrency 92
13.3 Virtual Reality and Augmented Reality 93
13.4 Quantum Computing 93
13.5 Real-World Applications 94

13.6 Practice test 95
Chapter 14: IT in Business and Society 98
14.1 Introduction 99
14.2 Digital Transformation 99
14.3 E-Commerce and Financial Technology (Fintech) 99
14.4 IT in Education, Healthcare, and Government 99
14.5 Challenges of Technology in Society 100
14.6 The Future of Work and IT Careers 100
14.7 Practice Test 101
References 104
About the Author 106

Chapter 1: Introduction to IT

1.1 What is IT?

Information Technology (IT) is a field of technology that deals with using computers, networks, and digital tools to handle information. In simple words, IT is all about creating, storing, processing, and sharing information with the help of technology. According to Schulze (2025), information technology is the practice of using modern tools and systems to overcome challenges, support the exchange of knowledge, and handle information in a way that improves efficiency and decision-making. We see IT in action every day. For example, when you use your smartphone to check emails, watch videos, or chat with friends, you are using IT. In the same way, businesses use IT to pay employees, keep track of products in their stores, talk with people across the world, and study data to make good decisions. IT is not just about computers. It also includes servers, cloud systems, mobile phones, apps, and internet connections that make it possible for information to move quickly from one place to another, and all these parts work together to make our digital world run smoothly.

1.2 Importance of IT in Daily Life

IT has become a fundamental part of our everyday lives. It impacts how we work, learn, communicate, and entertain ourselves. Online banking allows secure financial transactions from anywhere, while e-commerce platforms enable us to shop from home. In healthcare, IT systems manage patient records, schedule appointments, and even allow remote monitoring of vital signs. Transportation benefits from IT through GPS navigation, ride-sharing apps, and traffic management systems. During the COVID-19 pandemic, video conferencing platforms such as Zoom and Microsoft Teams became essential for work, education, and social interaction. Clearly, IT makes life more convenient, efficient, and connected.

1.3. Evolution of Information Technology

Information Technology (IT) has evolved rapidly over the past several decades, and transformed the way we live, work, and communicate. Hence, understanding the evolution of IT helps us see how technology has grown from simple tools to complex digital systems that power modern society.

Early Computing (1940s–1950s)

The first computers were large, expensive, and used mainly for scientific calculations and government purposes. These machines, like ENIAC and UNIVAC, were slow and required a lot of space and electricity. Input and output were done using punch cards and magnetic tapes. This era laid the foundation for all future IT developments.

Mainframe and Minicomputers (1960s–1970s)

In the 1960s, mainframe computers became popular in large organizations. They could handle multiple tasks and store larger amounts of data. Minicomputers followed, offering smaller and more affordable systems for medium-sized businesses. During this period, IT began to move beyond scientific research into business applications, such as payroll and inventory management.

Personal Computers (1980s)

The 1980s brought personal computers (PCs) into homes and offices. Computers like IBM PCs and Apple Macintosh made IT accessible to individuals. Users could now run programs for word processing, spreadsheets, and games. This era also marked the beginning of networking and early email systems, connecting computers within organizations.

The Internet and Networking (1990s)

The 1990s introduced the Internet to the public, revolutionizing communication and information access. Email, websites, and online services became common. Networking allowed computers to connect globally, making data sharing faster and easier. IT expanded from individual and business use to global connectivity.

Mobile Technology and Wireless Networks (2000s)

In the 2000s, smartphones, tablets, and wireless networks transformed IT once again. People could access information anytime, anywhere. Social media platforms emerged, and mobile applications became an essential part of daily life. IT became not just a workplace tool but a part of personal life.

Cloud Computing and Big Data (2010s)

Cloud computing allowed organizations to store and process data on remote servers instead of local servers. Big data technologies enabled businesses and researchers to analyze massive amounts of information for insights and decision-making. IT became smarter, faster, and more scalable in this era.

Artificial Intelligence and Emerging Technologies (2020s–Present)

Today, IT includes artificial intelligence (AI), machine learning, robotics, the Internet of Things (IoT), and blockchain. These technologies automate tasks, predict trends, and connect devices intelligently. Modern IT is no longer just about computing; it drives innovation, problem-solving, and new possibilities across all areas of life.

1.4 Types of IT

IT is a broad field with multiple interconnected areas, each one contributing to the functioning of modern technology. Understanding these types helps learners see how IT works in everyday life and professional settings.

Hardware

Hardware includes all physical components of a computer or IT system, such as desktops, laptops, servers, routers, printers, and mobile devices. Hardware forms the foundation for IT operations. Examples include a desktop computer in an office, a smartphone in your hand, or a server storing company data.

Software

Software consists of programs that tell hardware how to operate. System software manages hardware, while application software performs specific tasks. Examples include Windows 11 as system software, on the other hand, application softwares are Microsoft Word for writing documents, and Google Chrome for web browsing.

Networking

Networking connects multiple devices to share information and resources. Networks range from small home Wi-Fi setups to the global internet. Networking enables file sharing, communication, and internet access. For example, a home Wi-Fi network connects laptops, phones, and smart TVs, while a corporate network allows employees to access shared documents.

Data Management

Data management involves storing, organizing, and analyzing information to make it useful and secure. Databases and cloud storage systems are key tools in this area. Examples include hospitals maintaining patient records securely and Google Drive enabling file storage and sharing.

Cybersecurity

Cybersecurity protects systems, networks, and data from unauthorized access or cyberattacks. Common cybersecurity tools are firewalls, antivirus software, encryption, and security policies. Examples of cybersecurity include banks securing online accounts and employees using VPNs to safely access work networks remotely.

Cloud Computing

Cloud computing allows IT resources such as storage, servers, and software to be accessed over the internet rather than locally. Examples of cloud computing include Dropbox for file storage, Amazon Web Services (AWS) for cloud hosting, and Zoom for online meetings.

Artificial Intelligence (AI) and Machine Learning (ML)

AI enables machines to perform tasks requiring human-like intelligence, while ML allows systems to improve based on data. Examples include ChatGPT answering questions, Netflix recommending movies, and self-driving cars recognizing traffic signs.

Internet of Things (IoT)

IoT connects devices to the internet to collect and exchange data, and make life smarter and more automated. Examples of IoT include smart thermostats, wearable fitness trackers, and smart refrigerators notifying users when groceries are low.

Virtualization

Virtualization allows one physical device to run multiple virtual systems, improving efficiency and resource use. Cloud services often rely on virtualization. Examples of it include running multiple virtual machines on a single server or using Microsoft Azure to host cloud-based applications.

Programming and Software Development

Programming involves writing code to create software, apps, and websites. Examples include Python for data analysis, JavaScript for interactive websites, and mobile apps like WhatsApp for messaging.

Business IT and Enterprise Systems

This area focuses on IT applications supporting business processes, including ERP, CRM, and supply chain management systems. Examples include SAP ERP for inventory and finance management, Salesforce CRM for customer interactions, and Amazon's logistics software optimizing deliveries.

Emerging and Specialized Technologies

IT also includes cutting-edge technologies like blockchain, virtual reality (VR), augmented reality (AR), and quantum computing, which are transforming industries. Examples include blockchain enabling cryptocurrencies, VR used in gaming and training, and quantum computers performing calculations faster than traditional computers.

IT is a diverse and interconnected field. Each type plays a unique role, and together they create the systems, tools, and innovations that shape our digital world. Understanding these areas gives learners a clear view of how IT impacts daily life, business, and society, and prepares them to explore deeper concepts in future chapters.

1.5 IT Roles in Society

IT Helps Solve Everyday Problems

One of the most important roles of IT is solving problems. Computers and digital systems often face issues, such as software errors, network failures, or hardware malfunctions. IT professionals, such as help desk technicians and network engineers, work to fix these problems quickly. Their work ensures that offices, schools, hospitals, and even homes can function without interruptions. For example, if a company's online system crashes, IT experts troubleshoot the issue so employees can continue working without delay.

IT Improves Communication

Communication has become faster, easier, and more global. People can instantly send emails, make video calls, and share information through social media. Applications like Zoom, Microsoft Teams, and WhatsApp allow businesses, students, and families to connect from anywhere in the world. IT has removed distance as a barrier and makes communication instant and reliable.

IT Supports Education

IT has revolutionized education. Schools, colleges, and universities now use digital tools to enhance learning and teaching. Students can attend online classes, submit assignments electronically, and access study materials at any time. Teachers can create interactive lessons, track student progress, and provide immediate feedback using IT systems. This makes learning more efficient, flexible, and accessible for everyone.

IT Enhances Healthcare

Healthcare services are safer, faster, and more efficient with IT. Electronic Health Records (EHRs) store patient information digitally, which allows doctors to access medical history easily. Telemedicine applications enable patients to consult doctors online without visiting hospitals. Advanced software and artificial intelligence help in accurate diagnosis and treatment planning. Overall, IT improves the quality of healthcare and makes it available to more people.

IT Drives Business and Finance

Businesses and financial institutions rely heavily on IT for smooth operations. Online banking, e-commerce platforms, and enterprise software systems help companies manage resources, track performance, and serve customers efficiently. IT also helps businesses analyze data to make informed decisions, reduce errors, and increase productivity. From small shops to large corporations, IT is essential for modern business success.

IT Helps Governments and Public Services

Governments use IT to provide better and faster services to citizens. Online platforms allow people to pay taxes, apply for licenses, or access government services without visiting offices. IT also helps in managing traffic, monitoring public safety, and sharing emergency alerts. By using digital systems, governments become more transparent, efficient, and accessible to the public.

IT Protects Data and Security

As our world becomes digital, protecting information has become critical. Cybersecurity experts use tools like firewalls, antivirus programs, and monitoring systems to prevent hacking and data theft. IT safeguards personal, business, and government data from cyber threats, and ensures privacy and trust in digital systems.

IT Powers Entertainment

Entertainment has been transformed by IT. Streaming platforms like Netflix, online games, and virtual reality experiences allow people to enjoy movies, music, and interactive content anytime. IT makes entertainment more engaging, accessible, and interactive, catering to millions of users worldwide.

IT Supports Research and Innovation

IT is a key driver of research and innovation. Scientists, engineers, and businesses use computers, artificial intelligence, and cloud systems to analyze information, solve problems, and create new solutions. IT accelerates discoveries in science, medicine, technology, and other fields to drive societal progress.

1.6 Practice Test

Part 1: Multiple Choice Questions

1. What does IT stand for?

a) Internet Technology

b) Information Technology

c) International Telecommunication

d) Intelligent Tools

2. Which of the following is an example of IT in daily life?

a) Writing a letter by hand

b) Watching TV without internet

c) Checking email on a smartphone

d) Walking to a store

3. Which decade introduced personal computers to homes and offices?

a) 1950s

b) 1960s

c) 1980s

d) 1990s

4. Which of the following is a type of IT focused on protecting data from cyber threats?

a) Cloud Computing

b) Cybersecurity

c) Networking

d) AI and Machine Learning

5. Which technology allows multiple virtual systems to run on a single physical device?

a) IoT

b) Virtualization

c) Data Management

d) Programming

Part 2: True/False Questions

1. IT only includes computers and nothing else. (True/False)
2. Cloud computing allows you to access software and storage over the Internet. (True/False)
3. Email and video calls are examples of how IT improves communication. (True/False)
4. The first computers were small, cheap, and widely available to households. (True/False)
5. IT has no role in healthcare or education. (True/False)

Part 3: Short Questions

1. In your own words, define Information Technology.
2. List three ways IT impacts daily life.
3. Name two IT types and provide one example for each.
4. Explain one way IT helps businesses and finance.
5. Give one example of how IT supports research and innovation.

Answer Key (for Self-Check)

Part 1: MCQs Answers:

1-b

2-c

3-c

4-b

5-b

Part 2: True/False Questions Answers

1-False

2-True

3-True

4-False

5-False

Part 3: Short Questions Answers

1. IT is the use of computers, networks, and digital systems to create, store, process, and exchange information.

2. Examples: online banking, email, GPS navigation.

3. Hardware – desktop computer; Software – Microsoft Word.

4. IT enables businesses to manage resources, track performance, and make data-driven decisions.

5. Using AI to analyze research data or simulations.

Note on Answers:

The answers provided in this section are intended as sample solutions to help readers check their understanding of the material. They may not be the only correct answers, and variations or alternative solutions could also be valid. The author and publisher do not assume responsibility for any errors, omissions, or differing interpretations. Readers are encouraged to think critically, apply their own knowledge, and seek additional references where necessary.

Chapter 2: Understanding Computer Hardware

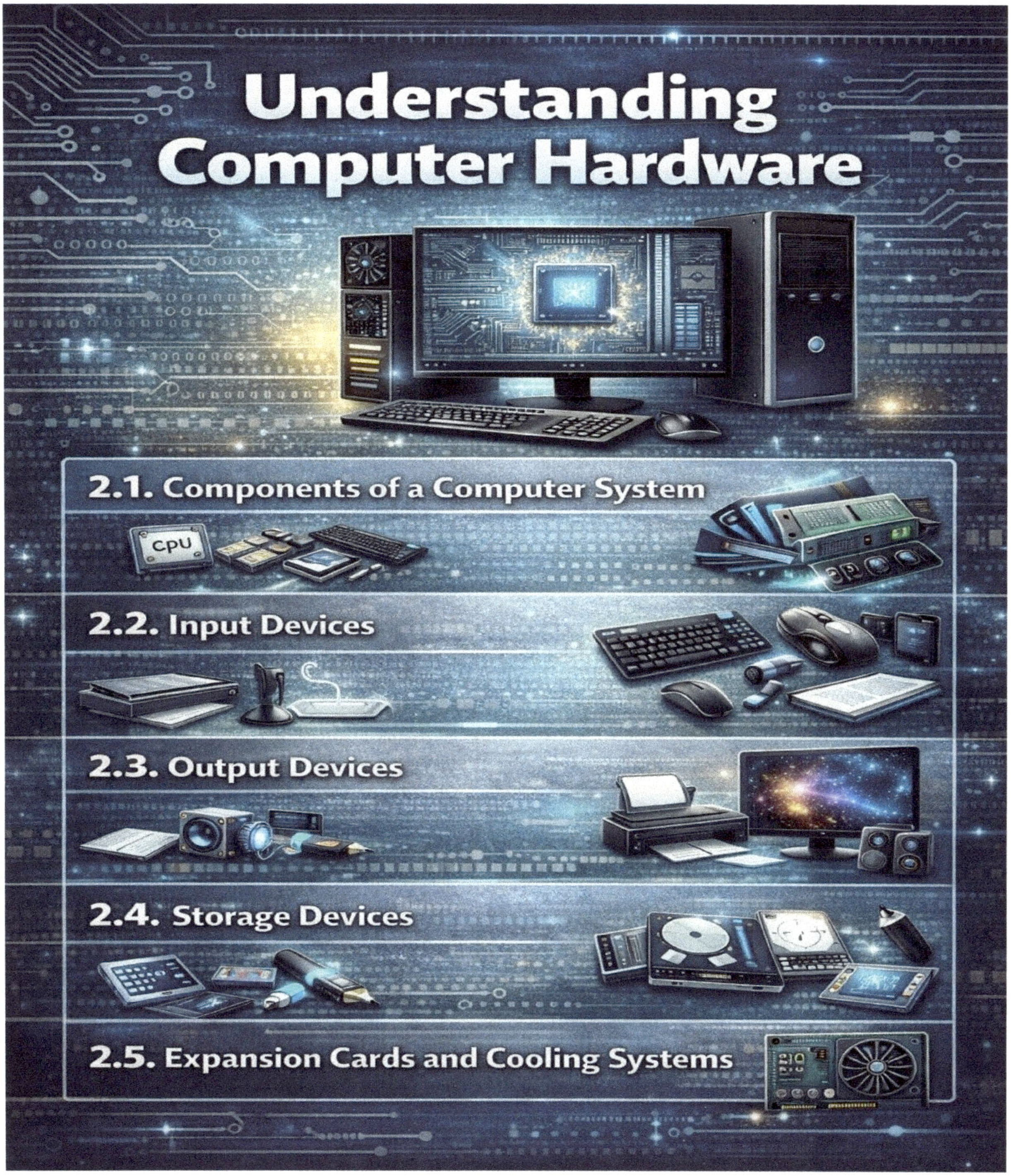

A computer is a machine that performs tasks by following instructions. It relies on hardware to work effectively, which is the physical parts you can touch. Hardware components process information, store data, take input from users, and provide output (Lanni, 2024). Understanding these components is essential for IT beginners because it helps with troubleshooting, upgrading, and using computers efficiently. This chapter explains the main hardware components, input and output devices, storage systems, expansion cards, and cooling mechanisms in detail.

2.1 Components of a Computer System

The main components of a computer system are:

- **Central Processing Unit (CPU)**
- **Motherboard**
- **Random Access Memory (RAM)**
- **Power Supply Unit (PSU)**
- **Peripherals**

The **CPU** is the brain of the computer because it controls all processing tasks. It executes instructions from programs and performs calculations. The Arithmetic Logic Unit (ALU) handles basic math operations like addition and subtraction, as well as logical comparisons like deciding whether one number is larger than another. The Control Unit (CU) manages how data moves between the CPU, memory, and other components. You can think of the CPU as a factory manager who oversees all operations and ensures tasks are executed correctly.

The **motherboard** is like the factory floor where all components meet. It connects the CPU, RAM, storage devices, and expansion cards. Without the motherboard, components cannot communicate and make the computer nonfunctional.

RAM is temporary memory that stores data actively used by the CPU. It is fast but volatile, which means all data is lost when the computer turns off. The more RAM a computer has, the more applications it can run simultaneously without slowing down.

The **PSU** provides power for the computer. It converts electricity from the wall outlet into the correct voltage for components like the CPU, motherboard, GPU, and storage devices.

According to Lanni (2024) **Peripherals** are devices outside the main computer that let users interact with it. Common examples include keyboards, mice, and printers. Without peripherals, inputting or receiving information from a computer would be very difficult.

2.2 Input Devices

The common input devices are:

- **Keyboard**
- **Mouse**
- **Scanner**
- **Microphone**
- **Touchscreen**
- **Other devices (game controllers, barcode scanners, webcams, fingerprint readers)**

Input devices let users send information and instructions to the computer. For example, a keyboard allows you to type letters and numbers, while a mouse helps you point, click, and drag items on the screen. A scanner converts a physical document into a digital file that can be edited or stored. Microphones capture audio for recording or online communication. Touchscreens allow you to directly interact with the screen by tapping or swiping. Other specialized input devices, such as game controllers, barcode scanners, webcams, and fingerprint readers, serve specific purposes in gaming, retail, security, and video communication. All these devices are essential for sending data to the computer efficiently.

2.3 Output Devices

Output devices include:

- **Monitor/Display**
- **Printer**
- **Speakers/Headphones**
- **Projector**
- **Other devices (haptic devices, Braille readers)**

Output devices allow the computer to communicate information back to the user. Monitors display text, images, and videos. Different technologies like LCD, LED, and OLED affect clarity, color, and brightness. Printers convert digital files into physical paper documents. Speakers and headphones allow the user to hear sound for music, notifications, or multimedia content. Projectors display visuals on large surfaces, ideal for presentations or classrooms. Specialized output devices, such as haptic devices, provide tactile feedback in simulations or games, while Braille readers help visually impaired users access text. Output devices make the computer's processing results understandable and usable for humans.

2.4 Storage Devices

The main storage devices are:

- **Hard Disk Drive (HDD)**
- **Solid-State Drive (SSD)**
- **Optical Discs (CDs, DVDs, Blu-ray)**
- **USB Flash Drive**
- **External Hard Drive**
- **Cloud Storage**

Storage devices are used to save data either temporarily or permanently. HDDs use magnetic storage to hold large amounts of data, such as movies, software, or documents. They are slower but cost-effective for high-capacity storage. SSDs use flash memory which makes them faster and more durable. They are ideal for running operating systems and applications that require speed. Optical discs, like CDs and DVDs, are mainly used for media storage or software installation. USB flash drives and external hard drives provide portable storage, while cloud storage allows users to save files online, and access from any device connected to the internet. Together, these storage devices ensure that data is safe and accessible whenever needed.

2.5 Expansion Cards and Cooling Systems

Expansion Cards (Graphics Card/GPU, Sound Card, Network Card)

Expansion cards add extra capabilities to the computer. A graphics card (GPU) improves video rendering for gaming, video editing, and 3D modeling. A sound card enhances audio quality, while a network card provides better connectivity for wired or wireless networks.

Cooling Systems (Air Cooling, Liquid Cooling, Heat Sinks)

Cooling systems are essential because computer components generate heat during operation. Overheating can cause errors or permanent damage. Air cooling uses fans to remove heat, while liquid cooling circulates coolant to absorb heat from high-performance parts like the CPU and GPU. Heat sinks are metal components that draw heat away from critical chips. Effective cooling ensures computers operate reliably and last longer.

2.6 Practice Test

Part 1: Multiple Choice Questions

1. Which component is known as the "brain" of the computer?

A. RAM

B. Motherboard

C. CPU

D. PSU

2. Which part of the CPU performs mathematical and logical operations?

A. Control Unit (CU)

B. Arithmetic Logic Unit (ALU)

C. Cache

D. Register

3. Which device is considered an input device?

A. Printer

B. Monitor

C. Speaker

D. Keyboard

4. Which storage device is the fastest and most durable?

A. Hard Disk Drive (HDD)

B. Optical Disc

C. Solid-State Drive (SSD)

D. CD-ROM

5. What is the main purpose of a Power Supply Unit (PSU)?

A. Store data

B. Cool the system

C. Convert and supply power

D. Process instructions

Part 2: True or False Questions

6. RAM stores data permanently even when the computer is turned off. (True/False)

7. The motherboard allows all computer components to communicate. (True/False)

8. A scanner converts physical documents into digital form. (True/False)

9. SSDs use magnetic disks to store data. (True/False)

10. Cooling systems help prevent hardware damage caused by overheating. (True/False)

Part 3: Short Questions

11. What is the function of RAM in a computer?

12. Name any two input devices.

13. What is the main difference between HDD and SSD?

14. Why are output devices important?

15. Give one example of an expansion card and its function.

Answer Key (for Self-Check)

Part 1: MCQs Answers

1. C

2. B

3. D

4. C

5. C

Part 2: True/False Questions Answers

6. False

7. True

8. True

9. False

10. True

Part 3: Short Questions Answers

11. RAM temporarily stores data and programs that the CPU is currently using.

12. Keyboard and mouse.

13. HDD uses magnetic disks and is slower, while SSD uses flash memory and is faster.

14. Output devices display or present processed information to users in a usable form.

15. Graphics card (GPU) – improves video and graphics performance.

Note on Answers:

The answers provided in this section are intended as sample solutions to help readers check their understanding of the material. They may not be the only correct answers, and variations or alternative solutions could also be valid. The author and publisher do not assume responsibility for any errors, omissions, or differing interpretations. Readers are encouraged to think critically, apply their own knowledge, and seek additional references where necessary.

Chapter 3: Software and Operating Systems

A computer cannot perform any task on its own. It needs instructions to know what to do, and these instructions are provided by software. According to the Hashemi-Pour (2024) software is a set of programs or instructions that tell the computer how to perform tasks. While hardware refers to the physical parts of a computer, such as the keyboard, monitor, or hard drive, software is invisible and exists as data stored in memory or on storage devices. Both hardware and software are required for a computer system to function effectively. Software is everywhere in our daily lives. From typing a document, sending an email, watching videos, or browsing the web, all these activities are possible because of software. Without software, even the most advanced computer hardware would be useless.

3.1 System Software

System software is the backbone of a computer system. It runs in the background and allows the computer to operate efficiently. This type of software is essential for the proper functioning of a computer, even though users may not directly interact with it.

The most important component of system software is the operating system (OS). The OS manages hardware resources, including the CPU, memory (RAM), storage devices, and input/output devices like keyboards, mice, and printers. It ensures that all hardware components and software applications work together seamlessly. For instance, when you open a file, the OS decides how to allocate memory and processing power to run the application. Another type of system software is utility programs. These are specialized tools designed to maintain and protect the computer system. Examples include antivirus programs, disk cleanup utilities, backup software, and system diagnostic tools. Utility programs help optimize performance, remove unnecessary files, and protect the system from security threats.

Device drivers are also a crucial part of system software. A device driver is a small program that allows the operating system to communicate with hardware devices. For example, a printer driver allows the computer to send print jobs correctly to a printer. Without drivers, hardware devices may not function properly, even if physically connected to the computer.

In short, system software acts as the invisible engine of a computer. It runs behind the scenes, ensuring that hardware and software can interact and that the system remains stable and secure.

3.2 Application Software

Application software is what users interact with directly. It is designed to help complete specific tasks such as writing, browsing the internet, editing photos, or playing games. Unlike system software, which runs in the background, application software provides tools for specific user activities.

Common examples of application software include Microsoft Word, used for writing and formatting documents, and Microsoft Excel, used for calculations and data organization. Web browsers such as Google Chrome or Mozilla Firefox allow users to access the internet. Photo editing programs like Photoshop help users manipulate and enhance images. There are also entertainment and communication applications such as Netflix, Spotify, WhatsApp, and TikTok. These applications provide functionality for streaming media, messaging, social networking, and gaming. Application software can be either free or paid, installed directly on your device, or accessed online as web applications.

Application software is essential because it transforms the computer into a useful tool for work, study, and entertainment. Without application software, a computer would not provide any real practical value to the user.

3.3 Operating Systems

The operating system (OS) is the most critical type of system software. It acts as a manager, coordinating hardware, software, and user interactions. The OS is the first program loaded when a computer is turned on, and it runs continuously until the computer is shut down.

The OS performs several key functions. It manages hardware resources like the CPU, memory, storage devices, and input/output devices. It also runs and manages applications and allows multiple programs to work simultaneously without conflicts. File management is another crucial function, as the OS organizes files and folders for easy access. Additionally, the OS provides security by managing user accounts and passwords and controlling access to sensitive data. The OS also provides a user interface, which allows users to interact with the computer. This interface may be graphical, with windows, icons, and menus, or text-based, using a command-line interface. Popular desktop operating systems include Windows, macOS, and Linux. Windows is the most widely used OS for personal and business computers, macOS is used on Apple devices, and Linux is popular among IT professionals and server environments.

On mobile devices, operating systems like Android and iOS manage device hardware, run mobile applications, and provide a smooth user experience. Without an operating system, a computer or mobile device cannot function.

3.4 Mobile Apps and Web Apps

With the growth of smartphones and tablets, mobile apps and web apps have become central to daily computing.

Mobile apps are installed directly on a smartphone or tablet. They are designed for touchscreens and downloaded from app stores such as Google Play or Apple App Store. Examples include WhatsApp, Instagram, TikTok, and Google Maps. Many mobile apps can function offline, meaning they do not need a constant internet connection.

Web apps run in a web browser and usually do not require installation. Examples include Gmail, Google Docs, and online banking platforms. Web apps often require an internet connection because they process data on remote servers.

The main difference between mobile apps and web apps is that mobile apps are installed locally on a device and can work offline, whereas web apps operate online in a browser and usually require internet access. Both types of apps have advantages and are widely used in education, business, communication, and entertainment.

3.5 Software Installation and Updates

Software must be installed on the device before using it. Installation is the process of copying the program files to the computer and preparing it for use. This process may include accepting license agreements, selecting installation options, and configuring settings. Proper installation ensures the software runs efficiently and does not conflict with other programs. Once installed, software must be updated regularly. Updates are important for several reasons:
Fix bugs: Correct errors that may cause the software to crash or behave incorrectly.
Improve performance: Make the software faster and more efficient.
Add features: Introduce new functionality or tools.
Enhance security: Protect against viruses, malware, and hackers.

For example, an outdated web browser may not display modern websites correctly and could expose the device to security risks. Many programs offer automatic updates to ensure the software remains safe and up to date. Regular updates are one of the simplest ways to maintain a secure and efficient system.

3.6 Practice Test

Part 1: Multiple Choice Questions

1. What is software?

A. Physical components of a computer

B. A set of instructions that tells the computer what to do

C. Only applications like games

D. Only system utilities

2. Which of the following is system software?

A. Microsoft Word

B. Google Chrome

C. Operating System

D. Photoshop

3. A device driver is used to:

A. Store files

B. Allow the OS to communicate with hardware

C. Make internet faster

D. Increase RAM

4. Which of the following is an example of a web app?

A. TikTok

B. WhatsApp

C. Gmail in a browser

D. Instagram

5. Software updates are important because they:

A. Only change the appearance

B. Add malware

C. Fix bugs and improve security

D. Slow down the system

Part 2: True/False Questions

6. An operating system runs only when you open an application. (True/False)

7. Mobile apps are installed from app stores and can work offline. (True/False)

8. Application software runs in the background and manages hardware resources. (True/False)

9. Utility software includes antivirus programs and disk cleanup tools. (True/False)

10. Without software, computer hardware is still fully functional. (True/False)

Part 3: Short Questions

11. What is the main purpose of an operating system?

12. Give two examples of system software.

13. What is a mobile app?

14. Why are software updates important? Name two reasons.

15. What is the difference between a mobile app and a web app?

Answer Key (for Self-Check)

Part 1: MCQs Answers

1. B

2. C

3. B

4. C

5. C

Part 2: True/False Questions Answers

6. False

7. True

8. False

9. True

10. False

Part 3: Short Questions Answers

11. The operating system manages hardware, software, files, security, and provides a user interface.

12. Examples:

Operating system (Windows, macOS, Linux)

Utility programs (antivirus, disk cleanup)

Device drivers

13. A mobile app is software installed on a smartphone or tablet, designed for touchscreens, and downloaded from app stores.

14. Software updates:

Fix bugs

Improve security

Add new features

Improve performance

15.A mobile app is installed on the device and can work offline. A web app runs in a browser and usually requires the internet.

Note on Answers:

The answers provided in this section are intended as sample solutions to help readers check their understanding of the material. They may not be the only correct answers, and variations or alternative solutions could also be valid. The author and publisher do not assume responsibility for any errors, omissions, or differing interpretations. Readers are encouraged to think critically, apply their own knowledge, and seek additional references where necessary.

Chapter 4: Networking Fundamentals

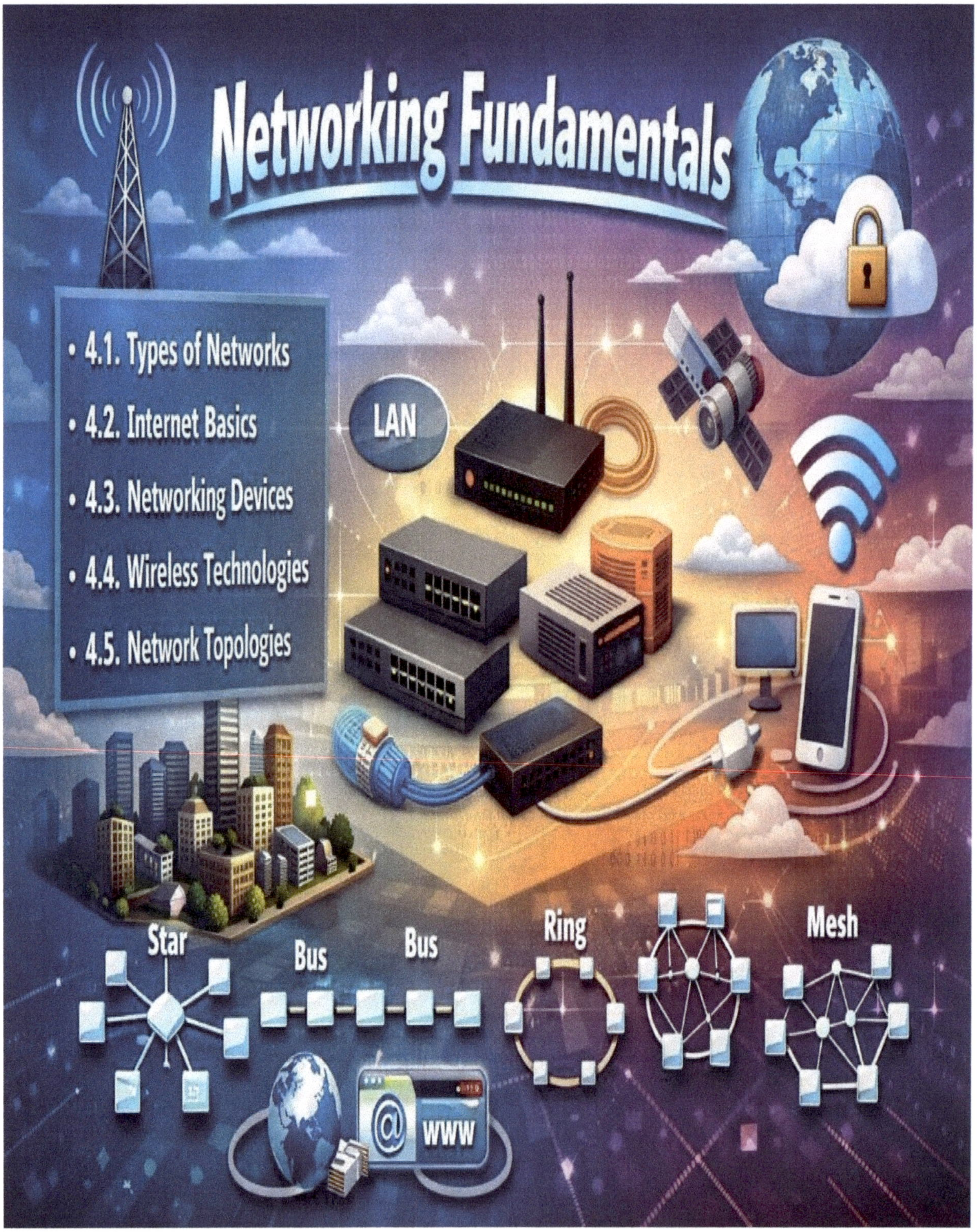

Networks are the backbone of modern computing. They allow computers, smartphones, tablets, and other devices to communicate, share information, and access resources such as the Internet. Almost every service we use today, including email, online banking, streaming, and social media, depends on a network. Understanding networking is essential for anyone learning IT because it provides the foundation for almost all digital communication.

This chapter introduces networking fundamentals in simple, practical language. You will learn about the different types of networks, key devices, wireless technologies, network layouts, and activities to help you understand how devices connect and communicate.

4.1 Types of Networks

A network is a collection of devices connected to share information and resources. Networks vary in size, purpose, and distance covered.

According to Petryschuk (2024) a **Local Area Network (LAN)** is designed for small areas such as homes, offices, or schools. Devices in a LAN connect using cables (Ethernet) or Wi-Fi. For example, computers in an office can share a printer or files easily.

A **Wide Area Network (WAN)** covers a large geographic area, such as multiple cities, states, or even countries. The Internet is the largest example of a WAN. Large companies often use WANs to connect their offices across different regions.

A **Metropolitan Area Network (MAN)** is larger than a LAN but smaller than a WAN, usually covering a city or town. Public networks connecting libraries, schools, or government offices in a city are examples of MANs.

A **Personal Area Network (PAN)** is very small and typically surrounds a single person. It connects personal devices like a smartphone, tablet, laptop, and wireless headphones, usually via Bluetooth or Wi-Fi.

Choosing the right network depends on scale and purpose. LANs are ideal for small areas, WANs for large-scale connections, MANs for city-wide networks, and PANs for individual use.

4.2 Internet Basics

The Internet is a global network of interconnected computers and devices. It allows us to access information, communicate with others, and use services like social media, email, online banking, and cloud storage.

Every device on the Internet has a unique IP address, which works like a house address, and allows data to be delivered accurately. Websites have domain names, like www.google.com, which are easier to remember than numeric IP addresses. To make communication possible, the Domain Name System (DNS) translates domain names into IP addresses.

For example, when you type www.google.com into your browser, your computer asks the DNS server for Google's IP address. Once it receives the address, your computer connects to Google's server, and the website loads. This process happens almost instantly and allows seamless access to websites worldwide. Think of DNS as a phone book. You know your friend's name, but not their address. DNS tells you the exact location so you can reach them. Without DNS, the Internet would be extremely difficult to navigate.

4.3 Networking Devices

Networks rely on various devices to operate efficiently. Each device has a specific role in ensuring smooth communication between computers, servers, and other networked devices. Understanding these devices is crucial for building, maintaining, and troubleshooting networks.

Router

A router is a device that connects a network, such as a home or office, to the Internet. It acts like a traffic manager, directing data to the correct device. When multiple devices request information from the Internet, the router ensures that the data reaches the right device. For example, when a laptop opens a website, the router sends the request to the Internet and delivers the website data back to the laptop.

Switch

A switch connects multiple devices within a Local Area Network (LAN). Unlike older devices, a switch sends data only to the device that needs it and prevents unnecessary network traffic. This ensures faster and more efficient communication. For instance, if a laptop sends a print job to a printer, the switch makes sure only the printer receives the data, rather than every device on the network.

Hub

A hub is an older network device that also connects multiple devices. However, it sends data to all connected devices, regardless of the intended recipient. This can cause network congestion and collisions, reducing efficiency. Today, hubs are rarely used because switches provide better performance and control.

Modem

A modem connects a network to the Internet Service Provider (ISP). It converts the signal from the ISP into a format that devices on the network can use. In effect, the modem acts as a bridge between the external Internet and internal network devices. For example, if the ISP provides Internet through a cable, the modem translates it into data that can be used by computers, phones, or other devices.

Access Point (AP)

An access point provides wireless connectivity and allows devices to connect to the network without physical cables. Access points are commonly used in offices to enable employees to access the network with laptops, tablets, or smartphones. Typically, an access point connects to a switch or router to extend the network wirelessly.

Office Network Example

In a typical office, a network is like the backbone that keeps everything running smoothly. Several devices work together to make sure employees stay connected and can share information quickly.

It all starts with the modem, which brings the Internet from the service provider into the office. Think of it as the doorway between the outside world and your office network, converting the signal into something your computers and other devices can use. From there, the router takes over. It acts like a traffic manager, making sure data gets where it needs to go—whether it's a document being sent to the printer, an email arriving at someone's computer, or a request to load a website. The router keeps everything moving efficiently, so there are no jams or delays. Inside the office, switches connect all the wired devices—computers, servers, printers and allow them to communicate quickly with each other. By handling the internal traffic, switches make sure the local network runs fast and smoothly. And for wireless devices, access points provide Wi-Fi coverage throughout the office. Laptops, tablets, and smartphones can connect wherever employees are working, giving them the freedom to move around without losing connection.

When these devices—the modem, router, switches, and access points—work together, they form a reliable office network that keeps everyone connected, whether they're on a wired desktop or a wireless device.

4.4. Wireless Technologies

Wireless networks allow devices to connect without the need for physical cables, providing flexibility and convenience. This technology enables devices to communicate over the air using radio waves or other wireless signals, and makes networking easier in homes, offices, and public spaces.

Wi-Fi

Wi-Fi is the most common type of wireless network. It provides Internet access over short distances using radio signals. Wi-Fi networks are widely used in homes, offices, cafes, airports, and other public areas, and allow laptops, smartphones, tablets, and other devices to connect to the Internet without physical connections. Wi-Fi technology is ideal for environments where mobility is important, as it allows multiple devices to share the same network seamlessly.

Bluetooth

Bluetooth operates over very short distances, typically a few meters. It is commonly used to connect peripherals such as headphones, keyboards, mice, smartwatches, and speakers. Bluetooth is designed for quick, low-power connections between devices and is especially useful for personal gadgets and wearable technology.

Cellular Networks (3G, 4G, 5G)

Cellular networks provide mobile Internet access for smartphones, tablets, and other portable devices. These networks have evolved over time, from 3G to 4G, and now 5G. Each generation offers improvements in speed, reliability, and connectivity. 5G networks, in particular, provide much faster data transfer rates and lower latency, and support modern applications such as high-definition video streaming, online gaming, and IoT (Internet of Things) devices.

Satellite Internet

Satellite Internet delivers connectivity to areas where traditional cable or fiber-optic connections are unavailable. It uses satellites in orbit to transmit and receive data and make it an essential solution for remote or rural locations. While satellite Internet may have higher latency compared to other wireless technologies, it enables users in isolated regions to access online resources effectively.

4.5 Network Topologies

According to Grassing (2024) network topology is like a plan or layout that shows how all the computers, printers, and other devices are linked together in a network - kind of like how roads connect houses in a neighborhood.

Bus Topology

Bus topology connects all devices to a single central cable. Data travels along the cable and reaches all devices, but only the intended recipient processes it. Bus topology is simple and cost-effective but can fail completely if the main cable breaks. Performance is also slow as more devices are added.

Star Topology

Star topology connects all devices to a central hub, such as a switch or router. Data passes through the hub before reaching the destination. Star networks are reliable because a failure in one device does not affect others, though a central hub failure would disrupt the network. Star topology is easy to manage, expand, and troubleshoot.

Ring Topology

Ring topology connects devices in a circular loop. Data flows in one direction from one device to the next until it reaches the target. While moderately reliable, a single device or cable failure can disrupt the network unless there is a backup system. Ring topology was more common in older office networks.

Mesh Topology

Mesh topology connects every device to every other device and ensures multiple paths for data. If one connection fails, data can take an alternative route. This makes mesh networks very reliable but complex and costly. They are often used in data centers and critical Internet backbone networks.

Hybrid Topology

Hybrid topology combines two or more topologies to leverage the strengths of each. For example, a large organization may use star topology within buildings and mesh topology to connect multiple buildings. Hybrid networks are flexible, scalable, and highly reliable which makes them suitable for large campuses and multinational organizations.

Choosing the right topology depends on network size, cost, reliability, and management needs. Small networks may use bus topology, offices often use star, and critical systems prefer mesh or hybrid networks.

4.6 Practice Test

Part 1: Multiple Choice Questions

1. Which network covers a small area, like a home or office?

(a) WAN

(b) LAN

(c) MAN

(d) PAN

2. What does DNS do?

(a) Connects devices to Wi-Fi

(b) Translates domain names into IP addresses

(c) Manages internal traffic

(d) Provides mobile Internet

3. Which device connects your network to the Internet?

(a) Switch

(b) Router

(c) Modem

(d) Access Point

4. Which wireless technology connects devices over short distances like headphones?

(a) Wi-Fi

(b) Bluetooth

(c) Satellite Internet

(d) 5G

5. In which topology are all devices connected to a central hub?

(a) Bus

(b) Ring

(c) Star

(d) Mesh

Part 2: True/ False Questions

6. A WAN can connect devices in different countries. (True/False)

7. A hub efficiently manages data traffic in a LAN. (True/False)

8. Mesh topology is reliable but expensive. (True/False)

9. An IP address is like a house address for your device. (True/False)

10. Wi-Fi provides Internet over long distances without a router. (True/False)

Part 3: Short Questions

11. Please give an example of a Personal Area Network (PAN).

12. Please explain the difference between a modem and a router.

13. Why is securing Wi-Fi important?

14. Please name two devices used to connect devices in a LAN.

15. What is the main purpose of network topology?

Answers key (for Self-Check)

Part 1: MCQs Answers

1. b) LAN

2. b) Translates domain names into IP addresses

3. c) Modem

4. b) Bluetooth

5. c) Star

Part 2: True/False Questions Answers

6. True

7. False

8. True

9. True

10. False

Part 3: Short Question Answer

11. Connecting smartphone, tablet, and wireless headphones via Bluetooth or Wi-Fi.

12. Modem connects to the ISP, router directs data within the network.

13. To prevent unauthorized access and protect data.

14. Switch and hub (switch preferred).

15. Determines how devices are arranged, affecting performance, reliability, and troubleshooting.

Note on Answers:

The answers provided in this section are intended as sample solutions to help readers check their understanding of the material. They may not be the only correct answers, and variations or alternative solutions could also be valid. The author and publisher do not assume responsibility for any errors, omissions, or differing interpretations. Readers are encouraged to think critically, apply their own knowledge, and seek additional references where necessary.

Chapter 5: The Internet

The Internet is one of the most influential technologies of the modern era. It acts as a global communication system that connects billions of devices across every country. From checking emails and browsing social media to running online businesses and accessing educational content, the Internet has changed nearly every aspect of daily life. Understanding how the Internet works is essential for students, IT professionals, and anyone who relies on technology. This chapter provides a detailed explanation of what the Internet is, how it functions, how devices locate each other, and how information travels across the world within seconds.

5.1. Understanding the Internet

The Internet is a massive worldwide network that links together millions of smaller networks. These networks belong to different organizations, universities, governments, and businesses, but all of them communicate using shared technical standards known as protocols. Because of these protocols, devices from different countries and manufacturers can exchange information smoothly. The Internet does not have a single owner; instead, it is a vast system maintained by thousands of network providers, engineers, and organizations. Its decentralized nature makes it resilient — even if one part of the network fails, the rest can still operate.

People use the Internet for countless activities. Communication is one of its most common uses, whether through email, messaging apps, or video calls. It is also a major source of information, offering millions of websites, online libraries, and learning platforms. Businesses use the Internet for online transactions, digital marketing, remote work, and customer service. Entertainment has also transformed, with streaming services, online gaming, and social networks becoming parts of everyday life. The Internet has grown into an essential global resource that supports social, educational, and economic development.

5.2. IP Addresses, Domain Names, and DNS

Communication on the Internet is only possible when devices can recognize and locate each other. This is where IP addresses, domain names, and DNS come in. Together, they form the addressing system of the Internet, similar to how physical addresses and phone numbers help people locate each other in the real world.

IP Addresses

An IP address, or Internet Protocol address, is a unique identifier assigned to every device connected to the Internet. It functions like a digital home address that tells other devices where to deliver information. When you request a webpage, send an email, or stream a video, your IP address helps the server know where to send the data. There are two main types of IP addresses: IPv4 and IPv6. IPv4 addresses are made up of four sets of numbers separated by dots, such as 192.168.1.10. Because the number of available IPv4 addresses is limited, a newer system called IPv6 was introduced and offers a much larger pool of addresses using longer combinations of letters and numbers. Without IP addresses, the Internet would not be able to route information correctly.

Domain Names

While IP addresses are essential for computers, they are difficult for humans to remember. This is why domain names were created. A domain name is a human-friendly label for a website, such as google.com or wikipedia.org. When people enter a domain name into their browser, they are actually requesting the website's IP address, but the browser handles this translation automatically. Domain names are organized in a structured way. The last part, such as .com or .org, is called the top-level domain. The word before it, such as "google" in google.com, is called the second-level domain. This structure helps organize websites in a logical and manageable way.

Domain Name System (DNS)

The Domain Name System, or DNS, acts as the Internet's address book. When a user enters a website's domain name, DNS translates that name into the correct IP address so the browser can reach the appropriate server. For example, when you type "youtube.com," DNS finds the exact numeric address of YouTube's server and directs your device to it. This process happens behind the scenes in milliseconds. Without DNS, users would have to memorize long numerical IP addresses and make the Internet far more difficult to use. DNS not only simplifies browsing but also ensures that websites remain accessible even if their server addresses change.

5.3. How the Internet Connects the World

The Internet works because countless devices communicate with each other using networking equipment, communication protocols, and physical infrastructure. Even though using the Internet feels effortless, every action you take triggers a complex series of steps behind the scenes.

At the core of Internet communication are servers and clients. Servers are powerful computers that store websites, applications, and data. Clients, such as smartphones and laptops, request information from these servers whenever a user wants to access something online. When a client sends a request, routers guide the data across networks so that it reaches the correct destination. Routers act like digital traffic directors and choose the best path for data to travel. Switches are used inside local networks, such as homes and offices, to connect multiple devices and help them communicate with each other efficiently. According to Strickland (2024) data does not travel in one large block, instead, it is broken into smaller units called packets, and each packet may take a different path to reach the destination server, depending on which network route is available. Once all packets arrive, the receiving device reassembles them into meaningful information such as a webpage, video, or message. This method makes the Internet fast and reliable, because even if one route is slow or unavailable, packets can travel through different routes to ensure the communication continues smoothly.

The Internet reaches devices through different types of connections. Fiber-optic Internet uses light traveling through thin glass fibers to deliver extremely fast speeds. Cable Internet uses the same infrastructure as cable television and is commonly found in homes. DSL Internet uses telephone lines and is slower compared to modern options. Mobile data, such as 4G and 5G, connects smartphones through cellular towers, and allows Internet access while on the move. In remote areas, satellite Internet provides connectivity through signals sent between the Earth and satellites in space. These different connection types work together to make the Internet accessible nearly everywhere.

5.4. The Importance of the Internet in Modern Society

The Internet has become a central part of modern living. In education, students and teachers rely on it for online classes, research materials, and digital assignments. It offers access to global knowledge and allows learning to happen from any location. In business, the Internet supports online shopping, digital payments, virtual meetings, marketing, and international trade. Many companies now operate remotely, relying completely on Internet-based communication and tools.

In communication, the Internet allows people to stay connected through email, video conferencing, social networks, and instant messaging. Families across the world can talk in real time and reduce the distance between them. Entertainment has also evolved dramatically. Movies, music, games, and live events can be accessed instantly through countless online platforms. The Internet has become a source of enjoyment and relaxation for millions of people.

Governments and healthcare services also benefit from the Internet. Online services allow people to pay taxes, apply for documents, and book appointments without visiting offices. Hospitals use the Internet for telemedicine, patient records, and remote consultations. Overall, the Internet is deeply woven into daily life and continues to shape how societies operate.

5.5 Practice Test

Part 1: Multiple Choice Questions

1. What is the Internet?

A. A single global computer

B. A network that connects many smaller networks

C. A type of software

D. A device used for communication

2. What does an IP address do?

A. Stores website passwords

B. Identifies a device on a network

C. Speeds up Wi-Fi signals

D. Translates domain names

3. What is a domain name?

A. A human-friendly website name

B. A type of Internet connection

C. A security tool

D. A fiber cable

4. What is the role of DNS?

A. Provides electricity to servers

B. Translates domain names into IP addresses

C. Creates new websites

D. Controls Internet speed

5. Which device directs data between networks?

A. Keyboard

B. Router

C. Printer

D. Scanner

Part 2: True/False Questions

1. The Internet is owned by one organization. (True/False)
2. Domain names are easier to remember than IP addresses. (True/False)
3. Fiber-optic Internet uses light to send data. (True/False)
4. All data on the Internet travels in one single big piece. (True/False)
5. Servers store information, and clients request it. (True/False)

Part 3: Short Questions

1. What is the Internet?
2. Why are IP addresses important?
3. What is the purpose of domain names?
4. What does DNS do?
5. What are data packets?

Answer key (for Self-Check)

Part 1: MCQs Answers

1. B

2. B

3. A

4. B

5. B

Part 2: True/False Questions Answers

1. False

2. True

3. True

4. False

5. True

Part 3: Short Questions Answers

1. The Internet is a global system that connects millions of smaller networks and devices.

2. IP addresses identify devices so data can be sent to the correct location.

3. Domain names make websites easier to remember compared to numerical IP addresses.

4. DNS translates domain names into IP addresses so browsers can locate websites.

5. Data packets are small pieces of data that travel separately across the Internet and get reassembled at the destination.

Note on Answers:

The answers provided in this section are intended as sample solutions to help readers check their understanding of the material. They may not be the only correct answers, and variations or alternative solutions could also be valid. The author and publisher do not assume responsibility for any errors, omissions, or differing interpretations. Readers are encouraged to think critically, apply their own knowledge, and seek additional references where necessary.

Chapter 6: Working with Data and Databases

6.1 Data, Information and Knowledge

Data is the foundation of all IT systems. By itself, data is simply raw facts or figures that have no context. For example, a list of numbers like 10, 20, 15 is just data—it does not tell you anything meaningful. When these numbers are put into context, such as "The temperatures over the past three days were 10°C, 20°C, and 15°C," data becomes information. Information has meaning and can be understood by humans. Information becomes knowledge when it is analyzed and applied to make decisions. For instance, seeing that the temperature rose significantly on the second day might lead a school to adjust classroom cooling. Understanding the difference between data, information, and knowledge is critical in IT, because it affects how data is collected, stored, and processed. A system that only stores raw data without converting it into useful information has a little value.

6.2 Structured, Unstructured, and Semi-Structured Data

Data can be classified based on its structure, which determines how it is stored and processed. There are three main types of data: structured, unstructured, and semi-structured.

Structured data is highly organized and stored in a fixed format, usually in rows and columns, which makes it easy for computers to process. Examples include spreadsheets, sales records, or student grades. For instance, a table of students with their names, ages, and grades allows a database to quickly retrieve information about any student. Structured data is ideal for relational databases because its organized format allows for efficient searching, sorting, and reporting.

Unstructured data, on the other hand, has no fixed format. It includes emails, photos, videos, social media posts, and audio files. Computers cannot easily read or analyze unstructured data without specialized software. Despite this, unstructured data is extremely valuable because it often contains insights about user behavior, preferences, or trends. For example, analyzing customer reviews on a website can reveal important feedback, but this requires advanced tools like natural language processing or AI.

Semi-structured data falls between structured and unstructured data. It contains some organizational markers but does not fit neatly into tables. Examples include XML files, JSON data, or log files. Semi-structured data is commonly used in web applications and APIs, where flexibility is important. For example, a JSON file containing student information may include different subjects for different students. This flexibility allows applications to handle diverse datasets without rigid database schemas.

6.3 Relational Databases (SQL)

Relational databases are designed to handle structured data efficiently. They organize data into tables, where each row represents a single record and each column represents a specific attribute of that record. Tables are connected through keys, which maintain relationships between different pieces of data. The primary key is a unique identifier for each row and ensure that no two records are identical. A foreign key connects one table to another and enables complex queries across multiple tables. The standard language used to manage relational databases is SQL (Structured Query Language). With SQL, users can insert new records, update existing ones, retrieve specific information, and perform complex analyses.

For example, in a student database, a table might look like this:

StudentID	Name	Age	Grade
101	John	15	9
102	Sara	14	8

Here, StudentID is the primary key. Using SQL, you could easily find all students older than 14: SELECT Name, Age FROM Students WHERE Age > 14.

Relational databases are powerful for applications where data is structured and relationships between data points are clear, such as banking systems, school records, or employee management systems.

6.4 NoSQL Databases

As the amount of data grew, especially with the rise of the internet and mobile applications, traditional relational databases faced limitations. Many applications now require handling large volumes of diverse, rapidly changing data. This led to the development of NoSQL databases, which provide greater flexibility and scalability. NoSQL databases do not require fixed table structures. Instead, they store data in formats like documents, key-value pairs, columns, or graphs, depending on the type of database. Document databases (like MongoDB) store data in JSON-like formats and allow for flexible fields. Key-value stores (like Redis) allow extremely fast access using unique keys. Graph databases (like Neo4j) store data as nodes and connections, making them ideal for social networks or recommendation engines. For example, a social media platform might store user posts, likes, and comments. Each post could have text, images, and videos. Because each post may have different elements, NoSQL databases can store this data efficiently without a rigid structure, unlike relational databases.

6.5 Data Storage Formats

Data storage formats determine how information is organized and saved so that it can be easily accessed, processed, or analyzed later. The choice of format depends on the type of data, the size of the dataset, and how the data will be used. Different formats serve different purposes — from simple text files to complex databases. Here you are going to learn the most common data storage formats and why they are used.

Basically, how data is stored depends on its type and intended use. Text files like CSV or TXT are simple and human-readable, suitable for small datasets. Binary files are optimized for performance and large datasets but are not readable without software. JSON and XML are semi-structured formats often used in web applications. Databases, whether SQL or NoSQL, provide structured storage with powerful querying and indexing capabilities.

Choosing the right storage format is essential for efficient data processing. For example, storing millions of social media posts in CSV files would be slow and impractical, whereas a NoSQL database can handle the same data efficiently and allow fast retrieval.

How Database Works

A database is like a digital filing cabinet that stores information in an organized way. We usually interact with it through a frontend, such as a website or application, where we enter or view data. However, what we see on the screen is only a small part of the system; the real work happens at the backend, where all the data is stored, organized, and managed. Data in a database is usually stored in an organized way so it can be easily found and used. Most databases store data in tables (rows and columns), like a spreadsheet. However, not all databases use tables — some store data as documents (like JSON files), key-value pairs (like a dictionary), or columns (used in big data systems). The format depends on the type of database and how it's designed to handle data. When we search for or request data, the database works behind the scenes to retrieve it efficiently. The frontend sends a query to the database, which looks up the information using its indexes and sends the results back.

In short, databases work behind the scenes to store, organize, retrieve, and safely manage data, and allow applications and users to access information quickly and reliably. The frontend shows the data in a user-friendly way, but the database is where all the real work happens.

6.6 Practice Test

Part 1: Multiple Choice Questions

1. Which of the following best describes data?

a) Processed information used to make decisions

b) Raw facts or figures without context

c) Knowledge applied in decision-making

d) A table in a database

2. Which of the following is an example of structured data?

a) Customer emails

b) Student grades stored in a table

c) Photos uploaded to social media

d) Audio recordings

3. Which type of data falls between structured and unstructured data, often using formats like JSON or XML?

a) Structured

b) Unstructured

c) Semi-structured

d) Relational

4. In a relational database, what is the primary key used for?

a) Connecting two tables

b) Storing unstructured data

c) Uniquely identifying each row in a table

d) Running NoSQL queries

5. Which database type is most suitable for handling large amounts of unstructured or rapidly changing data?

a) SQL

b) NoSQL

c) Spreadsheet

d) CSV file

Part 2: True/False Questions

1. Knowledge is simply raw data stored in a database.

2. Unstructured data cannot be analyzed at all.

3. JSON files are an example of semi-structured data.

4. Relational databases use tables with rows and columns.

5. NoSQL databases always use a fixed schema.

Part 3: Short Questions

1. Explain the difference between data, information, and knowledge in your own words.

2. Name two advantages of using relational databases.

3. Give one example of when a NoSQL database would be better than a relational database.

4. What is the main purpose of indexes in a database?

5. List three common data storage formats and briefly describe their use.

Answer Key (for Self-Check)

Part 1: MCQs Answers

1. b) Raw facts or figures without context

2. b) Student grades stored in a table

3. c) Semi-structured

4. c) Uniquely identifying each row in a table

5. b) NoSQL

Part 2: True/False Questions Answers

1. False

2. False

3. True

4. True

5. False

Part 3: Short Questions Answer

1. Data is raw facts (e.g., numbers or names). Information is data put into context (e.g., student grades for a class). Knowledge is understanding information and using it to make decisions (e.g., deciding to give extra lessons to students who scored low).

2. Advantages of relational databases:

Easy to query and retrieve data using SQL.

Relationships between tables allow for complex data analysis.

3. Example for NoSQL: A social media platform storing user posts, comments, and images where each post may have different fields.

4. Indexes make searching and retrieving data faster by organizing data for quick lookup.

5. Common storage formats:

CSV/TXT – simple, human-readable, good for small datasets.

Binary files – efficient storage for large datasets, not human-readable.

JSON/XML – semi-structured, often used in web applications for flexible data exchange.

Note on Answers:

The answers provided in this section are intended as sample solutions to help readers check their understanding of the material. They may not be the only correct answers, and variations or alternative solutions could also be valid. The author and publisher do not assume responsibility for any errors, omissions, or differing interpretations. Readers are encouraged to think critically, apply their own knowledge, and seek additional references where necessary.

Chapter 7: Cybersecurity Essentials

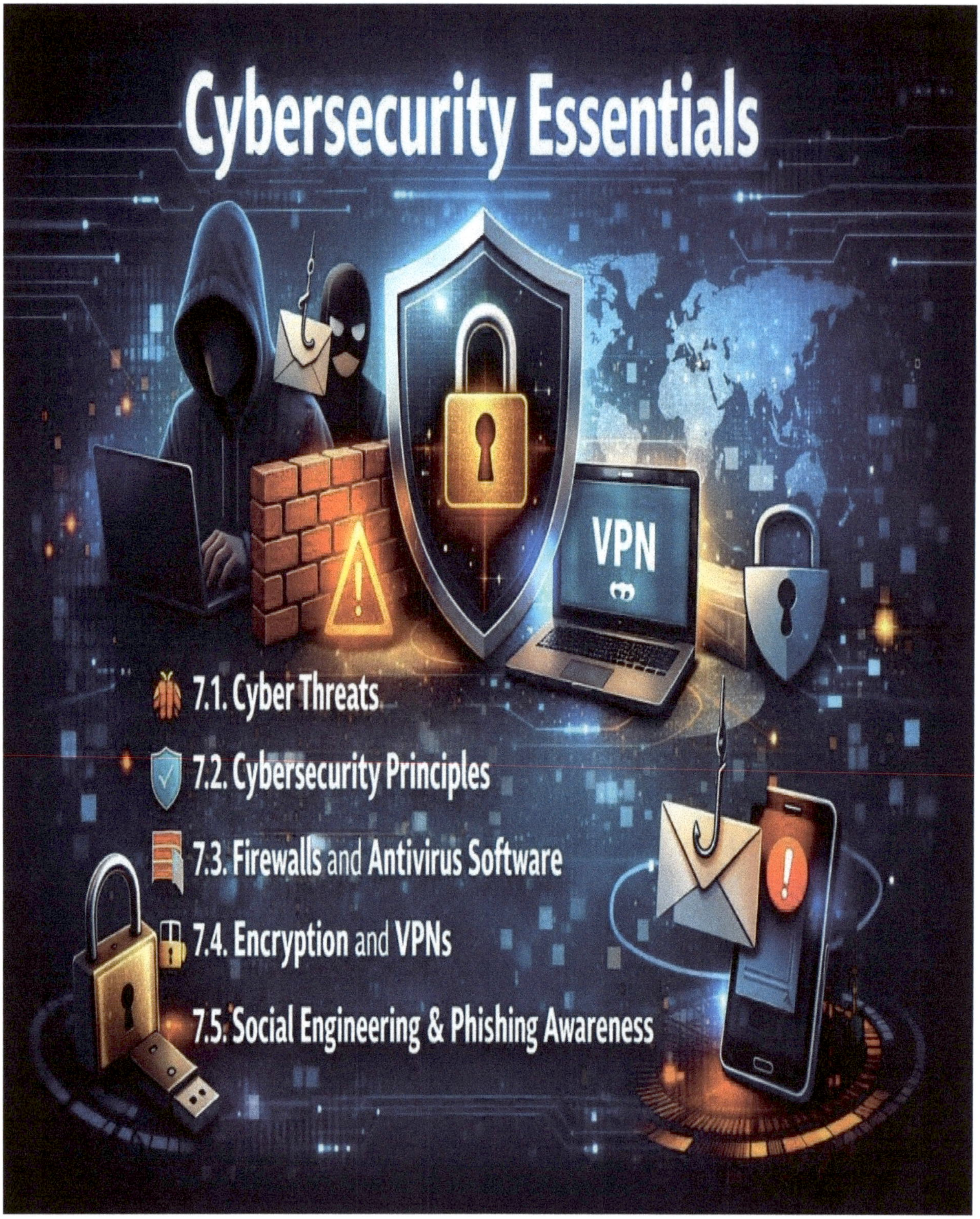

In today's interconnected digital environment, the protection of information and systems has become one of the most important challenges in the field of Information Technology. Cybersecurity focuses on defending computers, networks, and data from unauthorized access, damage, or disruption. As individuals, organizations, and governments increasingly depend on digital systems, understanding the basic concepts of cybersecurity is essential for ensuring the confidentiality, integrity, and availability of information.

7.1 Cyber Threats

Cyber threats refer to potential dangers that can compromise the security of information systems. These threats are often designed to steal data, disrupt services, or gain unauthorized access to networks. According to Baker (2024) cyber threats can originate from multiple sources such as hackers, organized crime groups, or even internal employees with malicious intent.

Common Categories of Cyber Threats

Malware: Malware is a general term for bad software that can damage your computer or steal your data. For example, a program might suddenly delete your files or make your computer run very slowly.

Viruses and Worms: Viruses and worms are programs that can spread from one computer to another. A virus needs a file to spread, while a worm can move across networks on its own. For example, downloading a file could infect your computer, and your friend's computer could also get infected.

Ransomware: Ransomware is a dangerous type of malware that locks your files and asks for money to unlock them. For instance, you might open an email attachment, and all your pictures and documents get locked with a message like, "Pay $200 to get your files back."

Spyware and Adware: Spyware and adware are programs that spy on you or show unwanted ads. Spyware secretly watches what you do online, like which websites you visit, while adware constantly shows pop-up ads on your computer.

Phishing Attacks: Phishing attacks are fake emails or messages designed to trick you into giving passwords, credit card info, or other private information. For example, an email might say, "Your bank account is blocked! Click here to fix it, but it's actually a scam.

Denial-of-Service: Denial-of-Service (DoS) attacks happen when hackers send too much traffic to a website or server, causing it to slow down or stop working. For example, you try to open a website, but it won't load because it's overloaded by an attack.

Cyber threats are constantly evolving, becoming more sophisticated as technology advances. Understanding these threats is the foundation of effective cybersecurity defense.

7.2 Cybersecurity Principles

Cybersecurity principles provide a framework for designing and maintaining secure systems. The most widely accepted model is known as the CIA Triad, which emphasizes three main components: Confidentiality, Integrity, and Availability. These principles guide how organizations develop security policies and strategies.

Confidentiality
Ensures that sensitive information is accessible only to authorized individuals.
Integrity
Protects data from being altered, damaged, or tampered with by unauthorized entities.
Availability
Guarantees that systems and data remain accessible to users whenever needed.

In addition to the CIA Triad, cybersecurity also relies on several supporting principles:
Authentication
Verifying the identity of users before granting access.
Authorization
Ensuring users have permission to access specific resources.
Accountability
Keeping records of actions to identify the source of any security incident.

These principles form the core of all security architectures and ensure that every system and process maintains a balance between protection and usability.

7.3 Firewalls and Antivirus Software

Cybersecurity depends heavily on technological tools designed to prevent and detect threats. Two of the most fundamental tools are firewalls and antivirus software.

Firewalls act as barriers between trusted internal networks and untrusted external networks, such as the Internet. They monitor incoming and outgoing data and block communications that do not meet established security criteria. Firewalls can be implemented as either hardware devices or software applications. They are typically configured with specific rules that define which types of traffic are allowed or denied and help prevent unauthorized access and data breaches. Antivirus software is another essential layer of defense. It scans files and programs to identify, isolate, and remove malicious code. Modern antivirus solutions often include advanced features such as real-time scanning, behavior monitoring, and automatic updates to protect against newly emerging threats. Keeping antivirus software updated is critical, as new malware variants appear daily. Together, firewalls and antivirus programs form the first line of defense against most common cyber-attacks.

7.4 Encryption and VPNs

Protecting the confidentiality and integrity of data during storage and transmission is a key concern in cybersecurity. Two important technologies that address these are encryption and Virtual Private Networks (VPNs).

Encryption is the process of converting readable information into a coded form that can only be deciphered by authorized users who possess the correct decryption key. It ensures that even if data is intercepted, it cannot be understood or used. Encryption can be applied to files, communications, or entire storage systems, and is fundamental in securing emails, financial transactions, and confidential records. VPNs provide secure communication over public networks by creating encrypted tunnels between users and remote servers. They protect the data transmitted across the Internet from being intercepted by attackers. VPNs are especially useful for securing connections in public Wi-Fi networks and maintaining privacy by masking the user's IP address and location.

Both encryption and VPNs are essential tools for maintaining privacy and preventing unauthorized data exposure in modern digital communication.

7.5 Social Engineering and Phishing Awareness

While technical measures are critical, human behavior often represents the weakest link in cybersecurity. Social engineering refers to manipulation techniques used by attackers to deceive individuals into revealing confidential information or performing actions that compromise security. Rather than exploiting software vulnerabilities, these attacks exploit human psychology.

Phishing is one of the most common social engineering attacks. It involves sending fraudulent messages that appear to come from legitimate sources and encourages users to disclose sensitive data such as passwords or financial information. Other forms include vishing (voice-based scams), smishing (SMS-based attacks), and pretexting (using false identity or scenarios to gain trust).

According to an IBM team, to prevent social engineering attacks, individuals and organizations must prioritize awareness and training, and recognize suspicious messages, verifying sources before responding, and following organizational security protocols are vital steps in defending against these threats. Human awareness and caution remain among the most effective defenses against social engineering.

7.6 Practice Test

Part 1: Multiple-Choice Questions

1. Which of the following best defines malware?

a) Software that helps improve system speed

b) Programs designed to harm or exploit computer systems

c) Security software that encrypts files

d) Hardware device for network management

2. The "I" in the CIA Triad represents:

a) Information

b) Integrity

c) Innovation

d) Identification

3. A firewall primarily:

a) Blocks unauthorized access to or from a network

b) Compresses files to save space

c) Encrypts all emails

d) Monitors user activity offline

4. Which type of cyber threat is specifically designed to lock users out of their files and demand payment?

a) Virus

b) Ransomware

c) Worm

d) Trojan

5. Social engineering attacks primarily target:

a) Operating systems

b) Hardware vulnerabilities

c) Human behavior

d) Network protocols

Part 2: True/False Questions

6. Encryption ensures that even if data is intercepted, it cannot be read without a decryption key. (True/False)

7. VPNs provide a secure connection over public networks by creating an encrypted tunnel. (True/False)

8. Antivirus software alone can prevent all forms of cyberattacks. (True/False)

9. Phishing is an example of malware that automatically infects a computer. (True/False)

10. Availability, in cybersecurity, ensures that authorized users can access information and systems when needed. (True/False)

Part 3: Short Questions

11. Define confidentiality in the context of cybersecurity.

12. What is the purpose of the CIA Triad?

13. Explain the difference between authentication and authorization.

14. Describe the function of antivirus software.

15. What is a firewall, and why is it important?

Answers key (for Self-Check)

Part 1: MCQs Answers

1. b) Programs designed to harm or exploit computer systems

2. b) Integrity

3. a) Blocks unauthorized access to or from a network

4. b) Ransomware

5. c) Human behavior

Part 2. True/False Questions Answers

6. True

7. True

8. False

9. False

10. True

Part 3: Short Questions Answers

11. Confidentiality means ensuring that sensitive information is only accessible to authorized users and protected from unauthorized access or disclosure.

12. The purpose of the CIA Triad is to provide the three core principles of cybersecurity — Confidentiality, Integrity, and Availability — to guide how organizations protect information systems.

13. Authentication verifies a user's identity (e.g., using a password), while authorization determines what that user is allowed to access or do once verified.

14. Antivirus software scans, detects, and removes malicious programs (like viruses, trojans, and worms) to protect a computer from infection.

15. A firewall is a security device or software that monitors and controls incoming and outgoing network traffic based on security rules. It helps block unauthorized access while allowing legitimate communication.

Note on Answers:

The answers provided in this section are intended as sample solutions to help readers check their understanding of the material. They may not be the only correct answers, and variations or alternative solutions could also be valid. The author and publisher do not assume responsibility for any errors, omissions, or differing interpretations. Readers are encouraged to think critically, apply their own knowledge, and seek additional references where necessary.

Chapter 8: IT Support and Troubleshooting

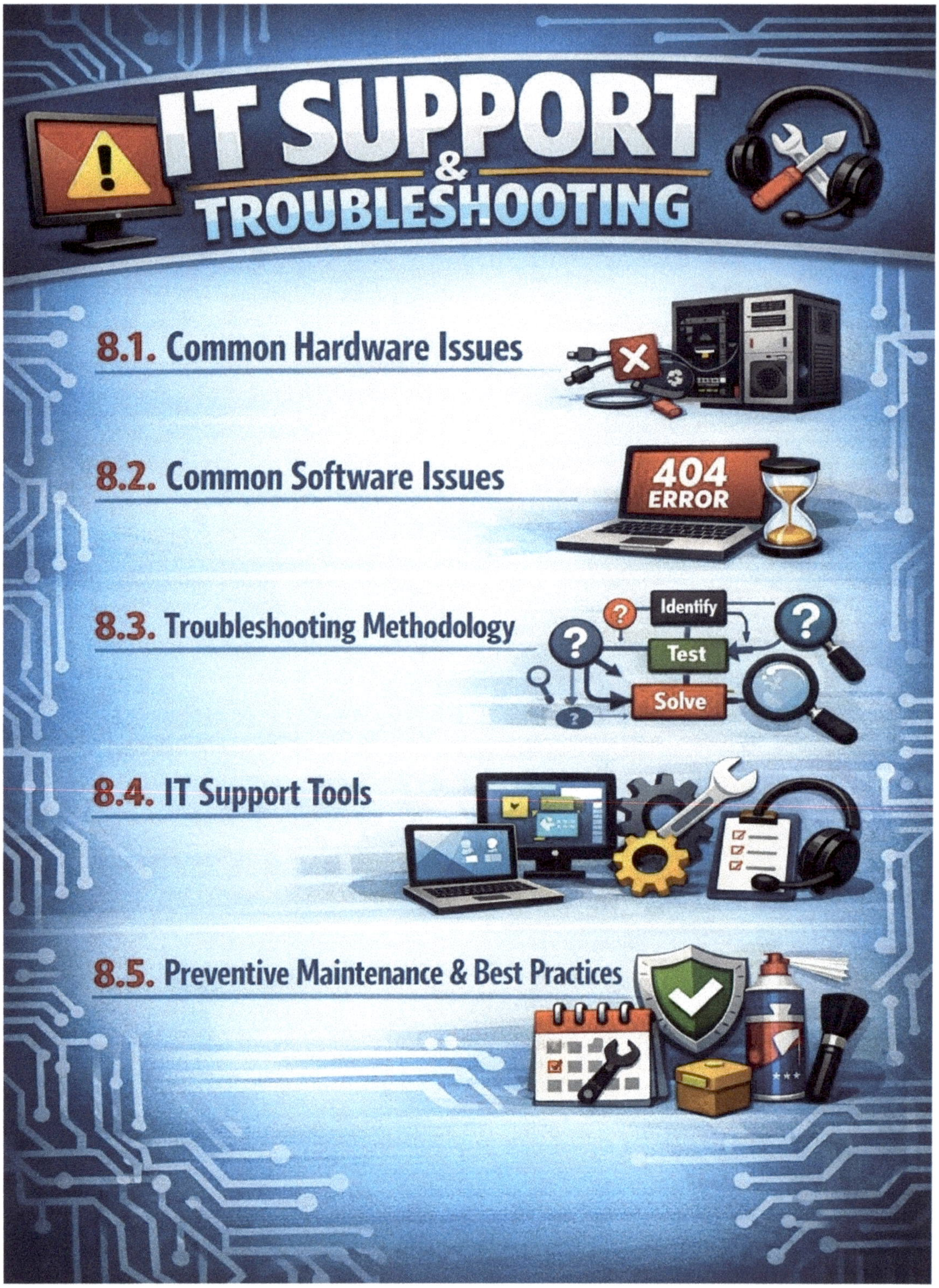

Technology is essential in modern life, and it's powering everything from offices and schools to hospitals and industrial systems. Despite its importance, technology is not infallible. Computers can fail to start, applications can crash, and networks can stop working. In such situations, IT support professionals play an important role. They diagnose problems, identify causes, apply solutions, and prevent issues from recurring. This chapter introduces the principles of IT support and troubleshooting, explores common hardware and software problems, presents a structured troubleshooting methodology, and highlights essential tools and best practices for maintaining reliable systems.

8.1 Common Hardware Issues

Hardware refers to the physical components of a computer system, including the motherboard, processor, memory, storage devices, graphics cards, and peripherals. Problems with these components can prevent a system from functioning correctly or even cause permanent damage if left unaddressed.

Power Failure

One of the most frequent hardware issues is power failure. A computer that will not turn on may have a simple problem, such as an unplugged cable or switched-off power strip, or a more serious issue, such as a defective power supply unit (PSU) or motherboard. Technicians begin by checking power connections, outlets, and switches, and may use a multimeter to measure voltage output. In cases of PSU failure, replacement is typically required.

Overheating

Overheating is another common hardware problem. Components such as the CPU and GPU produce heat during operation, and if cooling systems fail, this heat can accumulate, leading to random shutdowns, performance degradation, or component damage. Overheating is often caused by dust buildup, malfunctioning fans, or dried thermal paste. Preventive cleaning and proper airflow can significantly reduce overheating risks.

Display and Graphics Issues

Display and graphics issues often manifest as blank screens, flickering, distorted colors, or error messages like "No Signal." The cause may be loose or damaged cables, a defective monitor or graphics card, or incorrect display settings. Technicians systematically test each component, using alternate cables or monitors, and reinstall or update drivers as needed.

Storage Device Failures

Storage device failures can result in slow performance, errors, or data loss. Hard drives may produce unusual noises or fail to boot. Diagnostic tools such as CHKDSK or SMART monitoring help detect problems, while data backup and drive replacement are essential for data preservation.

Memory (RAM) Issues

Memory (RAM) issues are also common. Faulty or improperly seated RAM can cause crashes or blue screen errors. Technicians test RAM modules using software like MemTest86 and reseat or replace defective sticks. Peripheral devices, including printers, keyboards, and mice, frequently encounter connectivity issues or driver problems. Simple checks, reconnections, or driver updates often resolve these problems. Rarely, failures in the motherboard or processor may require professional replacement and are typically indicated by POST beep codes during startup.

8.2 Common Software Issues

Software problems can arise from corrupted files, misconfigurations, malware, or outdated systems. Unlike hardware failures, software problems often manifest as system slowdowns, application crashes, error messages, or abnormal behavior.

System Performance Issues

System performance issues frequently occur when too many programs run simultaneously, memory is insufficient, or malware consumes system resources. IT professionals use tools like Task Manager to identify high-resource processes, remove unnecessary applications, and scan for malware. Upgrading RAM or installing an SSD can also enhance system performance.

Application Crashes

Application crashes happen when programs terminate unexpectedly or become unresponsive. Causes include corrupted installation files, software conflicts, or incompatibility with the operating system. Solutions involve updating or reinstalling the application and checking system compatibility.

Operating System

Operating system errors can prevent booting, cause random restarts, or trigger error messages. Technicians use tools such as System File Checker (SFC), Deployment Image Servicing and Management (DISM), or System Restore to repair OS issues. If corruption persists, a complete OS reinstall may be necessary.

Driver Issues

Driver issues occur when hardware components cannot communicate effectively with the operating system. Outdated or missing drivers are common causes. IT support professionals check Device Manager, reinstall drivers, or update them to restore functionality.***Network and Internet Problems***

Network and internet problems arise from misconfigurations, faulty cables, or router failures. Troubleshooting includes verifying connections, using network utilities such as ping and ipconfig, restarting devices, and updating network drivers.

Malware Infections

Malware infections pose security risks and degrade system performance. Symptoms include pop-ups, file corruption, or unauthorized access. Addressing malware requires antivirus scans, removing infected files, and educating users about safe browsing practices. Similarly, the Blue Screen of Death (BSOD) signals critical system failures, often due to faulty hardware or driver conflicts. Identifying the error code, booting in Safe Mode, and replacing defective hardware are standard solutions.

8.3 Troubleshooting Methodology

Troubleshooting is a structured process that IT professionals follow to diagnose and resolve problems efficiently. A consistent methodology ensures that issues are addressed logically rather than through trial and error.

1. Identify the Problem: Gather detailed information from the user. Observe system behavior and note error messages, symptoms, and recent changes.

2. Establish a Theory of Probable Cause: Based on evidence, hypothesize what may have caused the problem. Multiple potential causes may exist.

3. Test the Theory: Conduct tests to confirm or reject the hypothesis. If the theory is incorrect, formulate a new one.

4. Plan a Solution: Once the cause is confirmed, devise a safe, effective repair plan. Consider the impact on the system and user data.

5. Implement the Solution: Carry out the repair, which may involve hardware replacement, software updates, or configuration changes.

6. Verify Full System Functionality: Test the system to ensure that the issue is resolved and no new problems have emerged.

7. Document the Process: Record the problem, diagnostic steps, resolution, and any follow-up recommendations. Documentation aids future troubleshooting.

8. Prevent Recurrence: Educate users, schedule regular maintenance, and implement preventive measures to reduce the likelihood of future issues.

8.4 IT Support Tools

IT professionals rely on a combination of hardware and software tools to diagnose and resolve problems efficiently. Hardware tools include multimeters for voltage testing, cable testers for network diagnostics, screwdrivers for hardware assembly, antistatic wrist straps to prevent static damage, POST diagnostic cards for motherboard errors, compressed air for cleaning, thermal paste for heat management, and external drive docks for testing storage devices. Flashlights and magnifiers assist in inspecting components.

Software tools are equally important. Task Manager monitors running processes, Device Manager identifies hardware issues, and Event Viewer provides detailed logs of system and application errors. System Restore allows recovery from problematic updates, while antivirus and anti-malware software protect the system. Network utilities like ping and tracert troubleshoot connectivity issues, and remote desktop tools enable offsite support. Diagnostic software such as MemTest86 and HWMonitor evaluate hardware health, while backup software ensures data protection during repairs.

8.5 Preventive Maintenance and Best Practices

Preventive maintenance reduces the likelihood of hardware and software failures and ensures system reliability and extending component life.

Hardware maintenance includes regular cleaning of dust from internal components, maintaining proper airflow, and monitoring component temperatures. On the other hand, software maintenance involves keeping operating systems, applications, and drivers up to date, applying security patches promptly, and performing routine system scans.

Data protection through regular backups, either on external drives or cloud storage, ensures that critical information is never lost. Users should also be trained in safe practices, such as avoiding suspicious downloads, emails, and unsafe websites.

According to Nash (2024) monitoring system performance and keeping records of errors, repairs, and maintenance schedules help IT professionals detect trends and potential issues before they become serious, and by combining technical expertise with preventive practices and user education, IT support ensures that technology remains reliable, secure, and efficient.

8.6 Practice Test

Part 1: Multiple Choice Questions

1. Which of the following is the most common cause of a computer that fails to power on?

a) Malware infection

b) Faulty power supply or unplugged cable

c) Corrupted operating system

d) Full hard drive

2. Which of the following is a primary symptom of RAM failure?

a) Printer not responding

b) Blue Screen of Death (BSOD) or random crashes

c) Flickering monitor

d) Network disconnection

3. What is the main purpose of MemTest86?

a) Scan for malware

b) Test RAM for errors

c) Monitor CPU temperature

d) Check hard drive health

4. Which step is part of a structured troubleshooting methodology?

a) Replace all hardware immediately

b) Identify the problem, hypothesize, test, implement, verify, document, prevent recurrence

c) Ignore minor errors

d) Restart the computer repeatedly

5. A computer that randomly shuts down without warning is most likely experiencing:

a) Malware infection

b) Overheating

c) Outdated drivers

d) Network misconfiguration

Part 2: True/False Questions

1. Overheating can permanently damage computer components. (True/False)

2. Peripheral device issues are always caused by software problems. (True/False)

3. Updating drivers is a preventive maintenance practice. (True/False)

4. Documenting troubleshooting steps helps in future problem-solving. (True/False)

5. Network problems can be caused by faulty cables, misconfigured routers, or driver issues. (True/False)

Part 3: Short Questions

1. Name two common causes of a computer failing to turn on.

2. Explain why overheating can affect computer performance.

3. List two common reasons for software applications crashing.

4. What is the purpose of using a multimeter in IT troubleshooting?

5. Why is preventive maintenance important for both hardware and software?

Answer Key (for Self-Check)

Part 1: MCQs Answers:

1. b

2. b

3. b

4. b

5. b

Part 2: True/False Questions Answers

1. True

2. False

3. True

4. True

5. True

Part 3: Short Questions Answer

1. A computer may fail to turn on due to a faulty power supply or unplugged cables.

2. Overheating can slow down performance, cause random shutdowns, and may permanently damage components like the CPU or GPU.

3. Software crashes can be caused by corrupted installation files or incompatibility with the operating system.

4. A multimeter measures voltage output to check if power is correctly supplied to components.

5. Preventive maintenance reduces failures, extends hardware lifespan, ensures reliable performance, and keeps systems secure.

Note on Answers:

The answers provided in this section are intended as sample solutions to help readers check their understanding of the material. They may not be the only correct answers, and variations or alternative solutions could also be valid. The author and publisher do not assume responsibility for any errors, omissions, or differing interpretations. Readers are encouraged to think critically, apply their own knowledge, and seek additional references where necessary.

Chapter 9: Programming Fundamentals

9.1. What is Programming?

Programming is the process of creating a set of instructions that a computer can execute to perform specific tasks (key, 2018). Computers do not have the ability to think or make decisions independently—they only follow instructions that are written in a precise manner. These instructions are written using programming language, which acts as a bridge between human logic and computer understanding. Programming is fundamental in today's digital world because it allows us to build software applications, automate tasks, analyze data, and even control smart devices.

Learning programming also teaches logical thinking and problem-solving skills. Every program you write requires you to break a problem into smaller, manageable steps and determine the correct order of operations. This ability to think logically and systematically is highly valuable not only in technology but also in everyday problem-solving. Programming is used everywhere—from simple tasks like creating a calculator to complex applications like artificial intelligence systems and online banking platforms.

9.2. Algorithms and Flowcharts

Before writing actual code, it is important to plan how a program will work. This is done through algorithms and flowcharts. An algorithm is a step-by-step set of instructions for solving a problem or performing a task. It ensures clarity and reduces mistakes when writing the program. For example, making a cup of tea can be represented as an algorithm: first boil the water, add tea leaves, steep for a few minutes, pour into a cup, and finally serve. This structured approach ensures that each step is executed in the correct order.

Flowcharts provide a visual representation of algorithms. They use standard symbols, such as rectangles for actions, diamonds for decisions, and arrows to show the flow of the process. Flowcharts are particularly helpful for beginners because they allow you to "see" the sequence of steps and understand the logic before writing code. For example, a simple flowchart for adding two numbers would start with "Start," then have steps for inputting the two numbers, performing the addition, displaying the result, and finally ending the program. Planning with algorithms and flowcharts makes coding much easier and more effective.

9.3. Understanding Programming Languages

Low-level languages are closest to computer hardware. They use numeric codes or simple commands that control memory and CPU directly. Examples include Assembly Language and Machine Language. These languages are fast but hard to read and are used in operating systems, hardware drivers, and embedded devices like car computers and medical machines.

High-level languages are easier to read and write because they resemble English. They hide complex hardware details, and allow programmers to focus on solving problems. Examples include Python, Java, C#, JavaScript, and Ruby. High-level languages are widely used for websites, mobile apps, desktop software, games, and artificial intelligence.

Scripting languages are small programs that automate tasks or add features to larger systems. Examples include Python, JavaScript, PHP, and Bash. They are used to automate repetitive work, manage files, or make websites interactive.

Object-Oriented Programming (OOP) languages organize code into "objects" that hold data and actions together. Examples include Java, C++, C#, Python, and Ruby. OOP is used in large software projects like banking systems, e-commerce platforms, ERP systems, mobile apps, and games.

Functional programming languages focus on using mathematical functions and avoid changing data, and make programs predictable and reliable. Examples include Haskell, Scala, and F#. They are used in finance, data analysis, AI, and scientific computing.

Declarative languages specify what the computer should do, without worrying about how. Examples include SQL, HTML, and CSS. SQL is used to query databases, while HTML and CSS structure and design web pages.

Markup languages help organize and format information. Examples include HTML, XML, and Markdown. They are essential in web development and data exchange between systems.

Domain-specific languages (DSLs) are made for specialized tasks. Examples include MATLAB for engineering, R for statistics, Verilog for chip design, and Regex for searching text patterns.

9.4. How and Where Programming Languages Are Used

Low-level languages are used in operating systems, device drivers, and embedded systems where speed and hardware control are essential.

High-level languages are used in websites, apps, games, AI, and automation. Python, Java, and JavaScript are especially popular for modern software development.

Scripting languages automates tasks and control systems. Bash scripts maintain servers, Python automates reports, and JavaScript makes websites interactive.

OOP languages are used for large systems like banking software, airline booking systems, e-commerce platforms, mobile apps, and games. They help multiple programmers work together efficiently.

Functional languages are used where accuracy and reliability matter, such as finance, data analysis, AI, and scientific computing.

Declarative languages like SQL, HTML, and CSS are used in databases and websites. SQL stores and queries data, while HTML and CSS structure and design web pages.

Markup languages structure and organize data. HTML creates webpages, CSS styles them, and XML transfers data between systems.

Domain-specific languages are used in specialized fields: MATLAB in engineering, R in statistics, Verilog in chip design, and Regex in text processing and cybersecurity.

9.5. Basic Debugging Techniques

Errors are a natural part of programming, learning to handle them is essential, and debugging is the process of finding and fixing errors in a program. Errors are generally classified into three types: syntax errors, runtime errors, and logical errors.

Syntax errors occur when the rules of the programming language are violated, such as forgetting a colon or parentheses. Runtime errors occur while the program is running, like dividing a number by zero or trying to access a file that does not exist. Logical errors happen when the program runs without crashing but produce incorrect results due to mistakes in reasoning or logic. Effective debugging requires reading error messages carefully, testing small parts of the program individually, and systematically isolating the problem. Writing clean, organized code and using comments to document steps also helps prevent and fix errors more efficiently.

9.6 Practice Test

Part 1: Multiple Choice Questions

1. Which of the following best defines programming?

a) Operating a computer

b) Creating a set of instructions for a computer to execute

c) Installing software

d) Repairing hardware

2. Which programming language is closest to computer hardware?

a) Python

b) Assembly Language

c) Java

d) Ruby

3. Which symbol in a flowchart typically represents a decision?

a) Rectangle

b) Diamond

c) Circle

d) Arrow

4. Which of the following is an example of a functional programming language?

a) Java

b) Haskell

c) Python

d) HTML

5. Which type of programming language specifies what the computer should do without describing how?

a) Low-level

b) Declarative

c) Scripting

d) Object-Oriented

Part 2: True/False Questions

1. Algorithms help programmers plan the steps of a program before coding. (True/False)

2. Runtime errors occur when the program violates the rules of the programming language. (True/False)

3. Object-Oriented Programming organizes code into objects containing data and functions. (True/False)

4. SQL is used to design the layout and style of a webpage. (True/False)

5. Debugging is the process of finding and fixing errors in a program. (True/False)

Part 3: Short Questions

1. What is the difference between a low-level and a high-level programming language?

2. Give one example each of a scripting language and a markup language.

3. What are the three main types of programming errors?

4. Why are flowcharts helpful in programming?

5. Name a domain-specific language and explain its use.

Answer Key (Self-Check)

Part 1: MCQs Answers

1. b) Creating a set of instructions for a computer to execute
2. b) Assembly Language
3. b) Diamond
4. b) Haskell
5. b) Declarative

Part 2: True/False Questions Answers

1. True
2. False
3. True
4. False
5. True

Part 3: Short Questions Answers

1. Low-level languages are closer to hardware and harder to read; high-level languages are easier to read/write and hide hardware details.

2. Scripting language: Python; Markup language: HTML

3. Syntax errors, runtime errors, logical errors. Flowcharts visually show the sequence of steps, helping to plan logic and prevent mistakes.

5. MATLAB – used for engineering calculations and simulations.

Note on Answers:

The answers provided in this section are intended as sample solutions to help readers check their understanding of the material. They may not be the only correct answers, and variations or alternative solutions could also be valid. The author and publisher do not assume responsibility for any errors, omissions, or differing interpretations. Readers are encouraged to think critically, apply their own knowledge, and seek additional references where necessary.

Chapter 10: Web Technologies

10.1. HTML, CSS, and JavaScript Basics

Web development is the process of creating websites and web applications, and it relies on three core technologies: HTML, CSS, and JavaScript. According to the Ubah (2021) HTML (Hyper Text Markup Language) provides the structure of a webpage, and defines elements such as headings, paragraphs, links, and images, and without HTML, a webpage would have no organization or content structure.

CSS (Cascading Style Sheets) controls the presentation and layout of a webpage. It defines colors, fonts, spacing, and how elements are arranged. CSS allows web developers to create visually appealing websites that match the design requirements.

JavaScript adds interactivity, and enables features such as animations, real-time updates, and form validations. Together, these three technologies form the backbone of modern web development and allow developers to create functional and attractive websites.

10.2. Frontend vs Backend

Web development is divided into frontend and backend development. The frontend includes everything the user sees and interacts with, such as buttons, menus, forms, and text. It is built using HTML, CSS, and JavaScript. The backend is the part of the website that runs on servers and manages data, user requests, and application logic. Common backend programming languages are Python, PHP, Java, and Node.js. For example, when a user logs into a website, the frontend displays the login form and buttons, while the backend checks the username and password in the database and sends a response back to the frontend. Frontend ensures usability and appearance, while backend ensures functionality and data processing. Both must work together seamlessly for a website to be fully operational.

10.3. Web Servers and Hosting

For a website to be accessible online, it must be stored on a web server, which is a computer that delivers website files to users when requested. Web hosting provides the infrastructure and resources necessary to run a website on the Internet. Hosting options include shared hosting, where multiple websites share the same server; VPS hosting, where a website has dedicated resources; and cloud hosting, which offers scalable resources for large or growing websites. Choosing the right hosting type ensures that a website remains fast, reliable, and accessible to visitors.

10.4. Responsive Web Design

With users accessing websites from desktops, tablets, and smartphones, it is essential for a website to adapt to different screen sizes. Responsive web design ensures that webpages adjust automatically to fit the device being used and provides an optimal viewing experience. Techniques for responsive design include flexible grids, scalable images, and media queries in CSS that apply different styles based on screen size. A responsive website maintains usability and aesthetics regardless of the device, which improves user experience and accessibility.

10.5. Content Management Systems (CMS)

A Content Management System (CMS) allows users to create and manage website content without writing code. CMS platforms provide templates, plugins, and user-friendly interfaces which make it easier to update and customize a website. Popular CMS platforms include WordPress, ideal for blogs and small business sites; Drupal, which is powerful for complex websites; and Joomla, offering a balance between simplicity and advanced features. Using a CMS saves time, reduces the need for technical knowledge, and enables users to focus on creating quality content while maintaining a functional website.

10.6 Practice Test

Part 1: Multiple Choice Questions

1. HTML is mainly used to:

a) Style webpages

b) Structure webpage content

c) Manage databases

d) Add animations

2. Which of the following CSS is responsible for?

a) Storing website data

b) Designing layout and colors

c) Running server logic

d) Creating user accounts

3. Which of the following JavaScript is mainly used for?

a) Structuring content

b) Adding interactivity

c) Choosing hosting plans

d) Creating servers

4. The backend of a website handles:

a) Buttons and menus

b) Colors and fonts

c) Database and server logic

d) Screen resizing

5. Responsive design ensures a website:

a) Works well on all screen sizes

b) Runs only on computers

c) Loads without the internet

d) Has more animations

Part 2: True or False Questions

6. CSS controls the style and layout of a website. (True/False)

7. HTML is used for making a website interactive. (True/False)

8. A web server stores and delivers website content. (True/False)

9. Backed development includes working with HTML and CSS. (True/False)

10. WordPress is an example of a CMS. (True/False)

Part 3: Short Questions

11. What does HTML do on a website?

12. Why do developers use CSS

13. What is the purpose of JavaScript?

14. What is a web server?

15. Give the name of one CMS platform.

Answer Key (Self-Checks)

Part 1: MCQs Answers

1. b

2. b

3. b

4. c

5. a

Part 2: True/False Questions Answers

6. True

7. False

8. True

9. False

10. True

Part 3: Short Questions Answers

11. It structures the content of a webpage.

12. To control design, colors, fonts, and layout.

13. To add interactivity (dynamic content, animations, form validation)

14. A server that stores and delivers website files to users.

15. WordPress / Joomla / Drupal.

Chapter 11: Mobile and Smart Technologies

11.1 Smartphones and Tablets

Smartphones and tablets have fundamentally transformed the way people interact with technology. These devices are more than communication tools—they are portable computers capable of running complex applications, accessing the internet, and integrating with a variety of services. A smartphone typically combines a high-resolution touchscreen, cameras, GPS, sensors, and internet connectivity, all managed by an operating system such as Android or iOS. Tablets, while similar in function, provide a larger display, which makes them particularly suitable for reading, media consumption, and productivity tasks such as document editing or digital drawing. The versatility of these devices has led to their widespread adoption in both personal and professional contexts and makes them essential components of modern IT ecosystems.

For IT professionals, understanding the architecture and operating principles of mobile devices is crucial. Knowledge of hardware components, operating systems, and app management enables them to troubleshoot problems, optimize performance, and provide secure solutions. The growth of mobile computing has also driven innovations in network management, app development, and cloud integration, highlighting the interconnected nature of modern technology.

11.2 IoT Devices and Wearable Technology

The Internet of Things (IoT) is a network of interconnected devices that communicate over the internet to collect, analyze, and share data. IoT devices have applications across diverse areas, from smart homes and wearable health monitors to industrial automation and environmental monitoring. By enabling real-time data collection and remote control, IoT improves efficiency, safety, and user convenience.

Wearable technology is a specialized segment of IoT that focuses on devices designed to be worn on the body. Smartwatches, fitness trackers, and medical monitoring devices continuously measure variables such as heart rate, steps taken, or sleep quality. These devices often connect to smartphones or cloud platforms and allow users to visualize trends and receive insights. IT professionals must understand how IoT devices and wearables communicate, manage data, and maintain security, as these devices often operate in highly interconnected networks where breaches or failures can have significant consequences.

11.3 Embedded System

Embedded systems are specialized computing devices designed to perform dedicated tasks. Unlike general-purpose computers, embedded systems are optimized for efficiency, speed, and reliability. They are integrated into a variety of technologies, including household appliances, automobiles, medical instruments, and industrial machines. Embedded systems operate with limited computing resources but are highly optimized for their specific applications.

Understanding embedded systems is essential for IT professionals because these devices form the backbone of modern smart technologies. Troubleshooting and maintaining embedded systems requires knowledge of both the hardware components and the software that drives them. For instance, a car's braking system relies on embedded microcontrollers to monitor wheel speed and apply braking pressure dynamically and ensure safety and reliability.

11.4 Mobile Application Ecosystems

Mobile applications, commonly known as apps, are software programs specifically designed for smartphones and tablets. They provide functionality for communication, productivity, entertainment, education, and many other purposes. Apps are typically distributed through official app stores such as Google Play and Apple App Store, which provide mechanisms for installation, updates, and security verification.

Understanding mobile application ecosystems is important for IT professionals because apps interact closely with device hardware and the operating system. IT personnel must ensure apps function correctly, remain secure, and are compatible with a range of devices. Furthermore, knowledge of app ecosystems supports troubleshooting, performance optimization, and guiding users in safe and efficient app usage. The app ecosystem is also a driver of innovation and enables developers to create new solutions that leverage the capabilities of mobile devices.

11.5 Device Communication

Mobile and smart devices rely on multiple communication protocols to exchange information. Wi-Fi enables high-speed internet connectivity within local networks, while Bluetooth supports short-range communication between devices such as headphones, wearables, and smartphones. Near Field Communication (NFC) facilitates contactless payments and device pairing, and cellular networks (3G, 4G, 5G) provide connectivity over long distances.

For IT professionals, understanding device communication is critical. Effective management of these protocols ensures seamless data transfer, connectivity, and security. For example, a wearable fitness tracker communicates with a smartphone using Bluetooth while simultaneously uploading data to a cloud service via Wi-Fi. Ensuring secure and reliable communication across such devices is a core responsibility in mobile technology management.

11.6 Practice Test

Part 1: Multiple-Choice Questions

1. What is the main purpose of a smartphone?

A. Only to make calls

B. To act as a portable computer with apps and sensors

C. To replace desktop computers

D. To be used only for gaming

2. Which device is an example of wearable technology?

A. Laptop

B. Smartwatch

C. Desktop PC

D. Router

3. What is an embedded system?

A. A general-purpose computer

B. A device designed to perform a specific task

C. A smartphone app

D. A cloud service

4. What is Bluetooth mainly used for?

A. Long-distance internet

B. Short-range device communication

C. Powering devices

D. Storing files

5. Which communication method is used for contactless payments?

A. Wi-Fi

B. NFC

C. Fiber optics

D. HDMI

Part 2: True/False Questions

6. Tablets have larger screens than smartphones. (True/False)

7. IoT devices usually communicate through the internet. (True/False)

8. Embedded systems are used only in phones and tablets. (True/False)

9. Mobile apps are usually downloaded from official app stores. (True/ False)

10. Bluetooth works for close-range communication. (True/False)

Part: 3 Short Questions

(Answer in 1–2 simple sentences.)

11. What is a tablet mainly used for?

12. What does IoT mean?

13. Give one example of a wearable device.

14. Why is security important for IoT devices?

15. What is NFC used for?

Answer Key (for Self-Check)

Part 1: Multiple-Choice Answers

1. B

2. B

3. B

4. B

5. B

Part 2: True/False Questions Answers

6. True

7. True

8. False

9. True

10. True

Part 3: Short Questions Answers

11. A tablet is mainly used for reading, watching videos, browsing, and productivity tasks on a larger screen.

12. IoT means Internet of Things — devices connected to the internet that share data.

13. Example: Smartwatch or fitness tracker.

14. Security is important because IoT devices can be hacked and they store or send sensitive data.

15. NFC is used for contactless payments and quick device pairing.

Note on Answers:

The answers provided in this section are intended as sample solutions to help readers check their understanding of the material. They may not be the only correct answers, and variations or alternative solutions could also be valid. The author and publisher do not assume responsibility for any errors, omissions, or differing interpretations. Readers are encouraged to think critically, apply their own knowledge, and seek additional references where necessary.

Chapter 12: Virtualization and Cloud Services

12.1 Virtual Machines and Hypervisors

Virtualization refers to the creation of a virtual representation of physical computing resources. A virtual machine (VM) is a self-contained environment that operates as if it were a physical computer, complete with its own operating system and applications. Hypervisors are specialized software programs that manage and allocate physical resources, such as CPU, memory, and storage, to virtual machines.

There are two primary types of hypervisors. Type 1 hypervisors, also known as bare-metal hypervisors, run directly on the hardware, and provide superior performance and security. Type 2 hypervisors, or hosted hypervisors, run on an existing operating system and are often used in testing or educational environments. Virtualization allows multiple operating systems and applications to run on a single physical machine which reduces costs and increases operational flexibility. This technology is foundational in modern IT infrastructure and enables efficient resource utilization and simplified management.

12.2 Benefits of Virtualization

Virtualization provides significant advantages in IT environments. According to Rivera (2023), it allows organizations to consolidate hardware, running multiple virtual machines on a single physical server, thereby reducing physical space and energy consumption. Virtual machines are isolated from one another and ensure that software failures or crashes in one environment do not affect others. Virtualization also facilitates rapid deployment and testing of new applications, as virtual environments can be created, modified, and removed without impacting physical systems. Additionally, virtualization enhances disaster recovery strategies, as virtual machines can be backed up and restored more efficiently than physical machines. These benefits make virtualization a critical component of modern IT operations

12.3 Cloud Storage and Local Storage

Cloud storage refers to storing data on remote servers accessed over the internet, while local storage involves saving data directly on physical devices such as hard drives or SSDs. Cloud storage provides the advantage of accessibility from any location, scalability for growing data needs, and redundancy for improved data protection. Local storage, on the other hand, offers faster access speeds, offline availability, and full control over data. IT professionals must understand the trade-offs between cloud and local storage, balancing performance, security, cost, and accessibility to design effective storage solutions for organizations and individuals.

12.4 Hybrid and Multi-Cloud Strategies

Modern organizations often adopt hybrid or multi-cloud approaches to achieve flexibility, reliability, and efficiency. Hybrid cloud environments combine private on-premises systems with public cloud services and allow sensitive data to remain secure while leveraging scalable resources for less critical workloads. Multi-cloud strategies use multiple cloud service providers to reduce dependency on a single vendor, improve redundancy, and optimize performance. These strategies require careful planning, integration, and monitoring to ensure seamless operation. IT professionals play a key role in implementing and maintaining these strategies and ensure that data and applications function reliably across multiple platforms.

12.5 Docker and Containerization

Containerization is a modern approach to software deployment that packages applications and their dependencies into portable units called containers. Unlike virtual machines, containers share the host operating system while remaining isolated from one another. This approach is resource-efficient and ensures consistent performance across different environments. Docker is one of the most widely used platforms for containerization, simplifying the development, testing, and deployment of applications. For IT professionals, containerization offers a practical solution for managing complex software ecosystems which enable rapid deployment, scalability, and consistent operation in both cloud and on-premises environments.

12. 6 Practice Test

Part 1: Multiple Choice Questions

1. A Type 1 hypervisor runs:

A. On top of an operating system

B. Directly on the hardware

C. Only in cloud environments

D. Inside a virtual machine

2. Which of the following is a benefit of virtualization?

A. More physical servers needed

B. Harder disaster recovery

C. Hardware consolidation

D. No isolation between systems

3. Cloud storage allows users to:

A. Access data only from one device

B. Access data over the internet from anywhere

C. Store data offline only

D. Avoid using the internet completely

4. A hybrid cloud combines:

A. Two public clouds

B. Only local storage

C. Private infrastructure + public cloud

D. Only one cloud provider

5. Containers differ from virtual machines because they:

A. Always require a full OS

B. Share the host operating system

C. Cannot run applications

D. Need separate hardware

Part 2: True or False Questions

6. Virtual machines are isolated, meaning one VM crashing does not affect others. (True/False)

7. Local storage requires an internet connection to access data. (True/False)

8. Multi-cloud means using multiple cloud service providers. (True/False)

9. Docker is a platform used for managing containers. (True/False)

10. Containers are heavier and use more resources than virtual machines. (True/False)

Part 3: Short Questions

(Answer in 1–2 sentences)

11. What is the main purpose of a hypervisor?

12. What is one major advantage of cloud storage?

13. Why do organizations use hybrid cloud environments?

14. What is virtualization used for in IT infrastructure?

15. What is Docker used for in containerization

Answer Key (for self-Check)

Part 1: MCQs Answers

1-B

2-C

3-B

4-C

5-B

Part: 2 True/False Questions Answer

6-True

7-False

8-True

9-True

10-False

Part 3: Short Questions Answer

11. A hypervisor manages and allocates physical hardware resources to virtual machines.

12. Cloud storage allows data to be accessed from anywhere with an internet connection.

13. Organizations use hybrid cloud to keep sensitive data on-premises while using public cloud for scalable workloads.

14. Virtualization allows multiple operating systems and applications to run on one physical machine, reducing cost and improving flexibility.

15. Docker is used to create, run, and manage containers that package applications with their dependencies.

Note on Answers:

The answers provided in this section are intended as sample solutions to help readers check their understanding of the material. They may not be the only correct answers, and variations or alternative solutions could also be valid. The author and publisher do not assume responsibility for any errors, omissions, or differing interpretations. Readers are encouraged to think critically, apply their own knowledge, and seek additional references where necessary.

Chapter 13: Emerging Technologies

The world of technology is always changing. Every few years when new inventions come, it completely transforms how we live and work. These inventions are called emerging technologies. They are still developing but already showing powerful effects in many fields. Technologies like Artificial Intelligence, Machine Learning, Blockchain, Virtual Reality, Augmented Reality, and Quantum Computing are shaping the future in ways that were once thought impossible. In this chapter, we will explore what these technologies are, how they work, and how they are changing our world.

13.1 Artificial Intelligence and Machine Learning

Artificial Intelligence, or AI, is when computers are programmed to think and make decisions like humans. AI allows machines to solve problems, recognize speech, and even understand emotions to some degree. For example, when you talk to Siri or Alexa, you are using Artificial Intelligence. It helps the device understand your words and provides an answer that makes sense. AI is used everywhere — in phones, cars, hospitals, and even social media apps.

Machine Learning, often called ML, is a branch of AI that helps computers learn from data and improve themselves without being programmed directly. Just like people learn from experience, computers learn by studying large amounts of information. For instance, YouTube learns what kind of videos you like and starts recommending similar ones automatically. In banking, Machine Learning is used to detect fraud by studying spending patterns. In healthcare, it helps doctors predict diseases earlier by analyzing medical records.

AI and ML are making life easier and work faster, but they also raise some challenges. People worry about privacy, data misuse, and how automation might replace some jobs. It is important that these technologies are developed responsibly, with rules that protect human rights and fairness.

13.2 Blockchain and Cryptocurrency

According to Rahman, (2024), blockchain is a technology that allows information to be stored securely and transparently across many computers. Imagine a chain made up of blocks, and each block holds a record of transactions. Once a block is added to the chain, it cannot be changed, which makes it very secure and trustworthy. Unlike traditional systems that rely on one central authority, such as a bank, blockchain is decentralized — meaning no single person controls it.

One of the most popular uses of blockchain is cryptocurrency. Bitcoin and Ethereum are digital currencies that use blockchain to record and verify transactions. People can send or receive money directly without needing a bank in the middle. But blockchain has many other uses too. It helps track products in supply chains so companies and customers can know exactly where goods come from. It can make voting systems more transparent, prevent fraud, and even protect digital identities from being stolen. Blockchain's greatest advantage is trust. It allows people to share information or money securely, even if they do not know each other. As more industries start using blockchain, it could change the way we do business, store data, and manage financial systems in the future.

13.3 Virtual Reality and Augmented Reality

Virtual Reality, or VR, creates a completely new world using computer graphics. When you wear a VR headset, you can feel as if you are walking on the moon, swimming under the ocean, or exploring a museum — all while staying in your room. It gives you the experience of being in a different place by using 3D visuals and sound.

Augmented Reality, or AR, is slightly different. Instead of creating a new world, it adds digital elements to the real world. For example, when you use your phone camera to play Pokémon GO or see how furniture looks in your living room through an app, that is AR. It mixes real and digital images together.

Both VR and AR are used in many ways. In education, they make learning more fun and interactive by taking students on virtual field trips. In medicine, doctors use VR to practice surgery before doing it on real patients. In retail, customers can use AR to try on clothes or makeup without visiting a store. These technologies make learning, shopping, and training more realistic and convenient.

13.4 Quantum Computing

Quantum Computing is one of the most advanced technologies being developed today. To understand it simply, regular computers use bits, which are tiny units that can either be a 0 or a 1. Quantum computers use something called qubits, which can be 0 and 1 at the same time. This special ability allows quantum computers to perform millions of calculations at once, solving problems that even the fastest traditional computers cannot handle.

Quantum computers could change many industries. In medicine, they could help scientists discover new drugs by quickly simulating how molecules react. In cybersecurity, they could create powerful encryption systems to protect sensitive information. In climate research, they could analyze complex weather data to predict natural disasters more accurately. Even though quantum computing is still in its early stages, its potential is enormous and could redefine the limits of computing in the future.

13.5 Real-World Applications

Emerging technologies are already shaping our daily lives. Smart homes use AI to control lights and temperature. Cars can now drive themselves with the help of sensors and machine learning. Doctors can monitor patients remotely through digital devices. Students can learn from anywhere using virtual classrooms.

However, these changes also bring challenges. Many people worry about job loss due to automation, privacy issues, and the growing gap between those who can afford new technologies and those who cannot. The future of technology depends on how responsibly we use it. It is important to balance innovation with ethics, so that technology helps everyone and not just a few.

13.6 Practice test

Part 1: Multiple Choice Questions

1. What is Artificial Intelligence (AI)?

A. A device that stores data

B. Technology that allows machines to think and make decisions like humans

C. A type of cryptocurrency

D. A virtual world created by computers

2. Which technology helps computers learn from data without being directly programmed?

A. Blockchain

B. Virtual Reality

C. Machine Learning

D. Quantum Security

3. What is blockchain mainly known for?

A. Editing videos

B. Secure and transparent record-keeping

C. Creating VR headsets

D. Designing mobile apps

4. Which of the following creates a completely computer-generated environment?

A. Augmented Reality

B. Cloud Computing

C. Virtual Reality

D. Blockchain

5. Quantum computers use which unit for processing?

A. Bits

B. Blocks

C. Tokens

D. Qubits

Part 2: True or False Questions

6. Machine Learning can recommend videos on YouTube based on your viewing habits. (True/False)

7. Blockchain can be changed any time after a block is added, making it less secure. (True/False)

8. Augmented Reality adds digital objects to the real world. (True/False)

9. Quantum computers are slower than regular computers. (True/False)

10. AI is used in healthcare, transportation, and smartphones. (True/False)

Part 3: Short Questions

(Answer in 1–2 sentences)

11. What is the main difference between Virtual Reality and Augmented Reality?

12. Why is blockchain considered trustworthy?

13. Give one example of how Machine Learning is used in daily life.

14. What is one benefit of quantum computing in medicine?

15. Name one challenge or concern related to emerging technologies.

Answer key (for self-check)

Part 1: MCQs Answers

1. B

2. C

3. B

4. C

5. D

Part 2: True or False Questions Answers

6. True

7. False

8. True

9. False

10. True

Part 3: Short Questions Answers

11. VR creates a fully digital world; AR adds digital objects to the real world.

12. Because once information is added to a block, it cannot be changed or controlled by one person.

13. YouTube or Netflix recommending videos/movies.

14. It can help discover new drugs by simulating molecules faster.

15. Privacy issues, job loss due to automation, or unequal access to technology.

Note on Answers:

The answers provided in this section are intended as sample solutions to help readers check their understanding of the material. They may not be the only correct answers, and variations or alternative solutions could also be valid. The author and publisher do not assume responsibility for any errors, omissions, or differing interpretations. Readers are encouraged to think critically, apply their own knowledge, and seek additional references where necessary.

Chapter 14: IT in Business and Society

14.1 Introduction

Information Technology has become the heart of modern life. It connects people, supports business growth, and helps governments and organizations work more efficiently. From online shopping and mobile banking to remote learning and telemedicine, IT has changed how society operates. In this chapter, we will learn how technology influences business and social life, what benefits it brings, and what challenges it creates.

14.2 Digital Transformation

Digital transformation means using modern technology to change how an organization works and delivers value. It is more than just buying new computers or software — it is about changing the way people think and work. When a company goes digital, it focuses on speed, efficiency, and better customer experiences. For example, many stores now sell products online instead of only in physical shops. Banks allow customers to transfer money using apps instead of standing in line. Hospitals store patient records digitally, which saves time and reduces mistakes. Even government offices are becoming digital, letting citizens pay taxes, renew licenses, or apply for services online.

Digital transformation helps businesses grow faster and become more efficient, but it also requires strong cybersecurity, employee training, and leadership that understands technology.

14.3 E-Commerce and Financial Technology (Fintech)

E-commerce means buying and selling goods and services through the internet. It allows customers to shop anytime, from anywhere. Websites like Amazon, eBay, and Alibaba make it easy to find products, compare prices, and have them delivered right to the door. For businesses, e-commerce reduces costs and reaches customers around the world.

Fintech, short for financial technology, is another major part of modern business. It combines finance and technology to make banking faster and more secure. Fintech includes mobile payment systems like PayPal, Venmo, and Apple Pay, as well as apps that help people invest or manage their savings. These tools make life easier but also require strong cybersecurity to protect personal and financial data from hackers.

14.4 IT in Education, Healthcare, and Government

Technology is transforming education by making learning more flexible and accessible. Students can attend classes online, use virtual labs, and access resources from anywhere. Teachers can reach more students and use digital tools to make lessons more engaging.

In healthcare, IT helps doctors diagnose diseases faster and store patient data safely. Telemedicine allows patients to consult doctors from home and reduces the need to visit hospitals in person. Technology also supports medical research by analyzing large amounts of data to discover new treatments. Government systems are also becoming more efficient with technology. Many countries now offer e-government services that let people pay bills, register vehicles, or apply for benefits online. This saves time, increases transparency, and reduces corruption.

14.5 Challenges of Technology in Society

While IT improves our lives in many ways, it also brings challenges. Privacy is one of the biggest concerns — people worry that their data may be collected or misused. Cyberattacks are another major issue, as hackers target banks, companies, and even governments. Automation has also replaced some traditional jobs, creating fear among workers.

To handle these challenges, society needs to focus on education, ethics, and cybersecurity. People must learn how to use technology safely, and governments should make fair rules that protect everyone's digital rights.

14.6 The Future of Work and IT Careers

Technology is changing the way people work. Many new jobs now require digital skills, and roles like IT support specialists, cybersecurity analysts, data scientists, and network engineers are in high demand. Even jobs outside of IT often require knowledge of computers and online systems.

The future workforce must be ready to learn continuously because technology never stops evolving. Professionals who keep updating their skills will find many opportunities. The key to success is not only using technology but understanding how it works and how it can be used responsibly.

14.7 Practice Test

Part 1: Multiple Choice Questions

1. What is digital transformation mainly about?

A. Buying new laptops for employees

B. Changing how organizations work using modern technology

C. Creating social media accounts

D. Hiring more workers

2. Which of the following is an example of Fintech?

A. Google Maps

B. PayPal

C. Photoshop

D. Microsoft Word

3. Telemedicine allows patients to:

A. Travel to hospitals faster

B. Consult doctors online from home

C. Buy medicine from vending machines

D. Create their own digital medical records

4. What is one benefit of e-government services?

A. Only work during office hours

B. Requires no cybersecurity

C. Saves time by letting people access services online

D. Makes government less transparent

5. Which IT career is becoming highly in demand?

A. Candle maker

B. Cybersecurity analyst

C. Taxi dispatcher

D. Librarian assistant

Part 3: True/False Questions

6. Digital transformation focuses only on using computers, not on changing work processes.

7. E-commerce allows customers to shop anytime from anywhere.

8. Automation has replaced some traditional jobs.

9. Fintech systems do not require cybersecurity protection.

10. IT helps governments offer faster and more transparent services.

Part 4: Short Questions

(Answer in 1–2 sentences)

11. What is e-commerce?

12. How does technology improve education?

13. Why is cybersecurity important for Fintech?

14. Name one challenge society faces due to technology.

15. Why must the future workforce continue learning new skills?

Answer Key (for self-Check)

Part 1: MCQs Answers

1. B

2. B

3. B

4. C

5. B

Part 2: True/False Questions Answer

6. False

7. True

8. True

9. False

10. True

Part 3: Short Questions Answers

11. Buying and selling goods or services over the internet.

12. It makes learning flexible, allows online classes, and provides digital tools for students and teachers.

13. Because financial data is sensitive and hackers often target payment systems.

14. Privacy issues, cyberattacks, or job loss due to automation.

15. Because technology changes quickly and jobs require updated digital skills.

Note on Answers:

The answers provided in this section are intended as sample solutions to help readers check their understanding of the material. They may not be the only correct answers, and variations or alternative solutions could also be valid. The author and publisher do not assume responsibility for any errors, omissions, or differing interpretations. Readers are encouraged to think critically, apply their own knowledge, and seek additional references where necessary.

References

Schulze, J. (2025). What is Information Technology? 2025 Guide. *Coursera.* https://www.coursera.org/articles/what-is-information-technology

Lanni, R. (2024, January 29). Basic computer hardware - learn the essentials. *Lincoln Tech Blog* https://www.lincolntech.edu/news/information-technology/basic-computer-hardware-essentials networking-student

Freiburger, P. A., & Swaine, M. R. (2025, September 24). Computer.*Encyclopaedia Britannica, Inc.* https://www.britannica.com/technology/computer

OpenAI. (2025). ChatGPT [Large language model]. *OpenAI.*https://chat.openai.com/

Susnjara, S., & Smalley, I. (n.d.). What is an operating system? *IBM.* https://www.ibm.com/think/topics/operating-systems

Hashemi-Pour, C. (2024, June 6). What is software? *TechTarget.* https://techtarget.com/searchapparchitecture/definition/software

Petryschuk, S. (2024, October 24). 11 types of networks: Understanding the differences. *Auvik.* https://www.auvik.com/franklyit/blog/types-of-networks/

Grassing, R. (2024, August 19). What is network topology? Definition and overview of types. *Auvik.* https://www.auvik.com/franklyit/blog/what-is-network-topology/

Strickland, J. (2024, May 17). How does the Internet work? *HowStuffWorks.* https://computer.howstuffworks.com/internet/basics/internet.htm

Dasari, P. (2023, October 31st). Role of Internet Communication in Modern Society. *Vitel Global Communications.* https://www.vitelglobal.com/blog/internet-communication-in-modern-society/

Spilker, J. (2024, October 15). Data vs Information vs Knowledge: What are the differences? *tettra.com* https://tettra.com/article/data-vs-information-vs-knowledge-what-are-the-differences/

Kosinski, M. (n.d.). What is a database? *IBM.* https://www.ibm.com/think/topics/database

Baker, K. (2024, May 12).12 most common types of cyberattacks. *CrowdStrike.* https://www.crowdstrike.com/en-us/cybersecurity-101/cyberattacks/common-cyberattacks/

IBM Cloud Team. (n.d.). Types of cyberthreats. *IBM.*https://www.ibm.com/think/topics/cyberthreats-types

Westerlund, W. (2024, September 4). IT help desk & support troubleshooting guide. *Suptask.* https://www.suptask.com/blog/help-desk-troubleshooting-guide

Nash, A. (2024, May 8). 50 most common IT support problems and their solutions. *itadon.com.* https://itadon.com/blog/50-most-common-it-support-problems-and-their-solutions

Kay, R. M. (2018, December 24). Programming Fundamentals Part 1: What is a program? *Medium*.https://rkay301.medium.com/programming-fundamentals-part-one-what-is-a-program-6e6639aedc58

Plantz, R. G. (n.d.). Introduction to Computer Organization: ARM Assembly Language Using the Raspberry Pi. Retrieved from https://bob.cs.sonoma.edu/testing/sec-progorg.html

Larsen, R. (2013). Beginning HTML and CSS *Wrox*.https://www.oreilly.com/library/view/beginning-html-and/9781118416518/c10.html

Ubah, K. (2021, August 10). Learn web development basics - HTML, CSS, and JavaScript explained for beginners. *FreeCodeCamp*.https://www.freecodecamp.org/news/html-css-and-javascript-explained-for-beginners/

Monga, S. (n.d.). Mobile technology: Meaning, types, uses, advantages and more. Plutus Education. Retrieved November 22, 2025, from https://plutuseducation.com/blog/smart-technologies/

Goddard, W. (2021, May 19). Mobile technologies. *IT Chronicles* https://itchronicles.com/mobile/mobile-technologies/

Rivera, A. (2023, October 23). Virtualization vs. cloud computing: What's the difference? *Business News Daily*.https://www.businessnewsdaily.com/5791-virtualization-vs-cloud-computing.html

Griesemer, M. (n.d.). What is the difference between virtualization and cloud computing? Citrix Blogs. Retrieved December 2, 2025, from https://www.citrix.com/blogs/2022/08/10/difference-between-virtualization-and-cloud-computing/amp/

Zeichick, A. (2025, April 10). What is cloud computing? Oracle. https://www.oracle.com/cloud/what-is-cloud-computing/

Rahman, M. M. (2024, September 23) Emerging Technology: Key Challenges and Opportunities. *ISACA*.https://www.isaca.org/resources/news-and-trends/newsletters/atisaca/2024/volume-17/emerging-technology-key-challenges-and-opportunities

Duggal, N. (2025, October 30). 20 New Technology Trends for 2026. *Simplilearn*.https://www.simplilearn.com/top-technology-trends-and-jobs-article

Zwass, V. (2025, November 21). Information systems in the economy and society. *Encyclopedia Britannica* https://www.britannica.com/topic/information-system/Information-systems-in-the-economy-and-society

Harding, C. (2017, November 6). Integrating IT with Business and Society. *Compare the Cloud.* https://www.comparethecloud.net/articles/integrating-it-with-business-and-society/

About the Author

Sha Md Farid is a business-driven IT professional, researcher, and emerging figure in academia with a strong interdisciplinary foundation in both business and information technology. He holds a Bachelor's Degree in Business Administration from Woosong University, South Korea, and a Master of Science in Information Systems Technology with a concentration in Information Assurance from Wilmington University, USA.

Farid's expertise covers network security, data security, cloud Security, web and application security, and the practical application of machine learning across diverse domains. He has co-authored several peer-reviewed research papers and has presented his work at international conferences, focusing on how modern IT and cybersecurity solutions can address real-world challenges.

In Fundamentals of Information Technology- A Comprehensive Guide, Farid translates complex technical concepts into clear, structured, and beginner-friendly explanations. Designed for complete beginners as well as learners seeking to strengthen their foundational knowledge, this book offers a guided journey from core IT principles to the essential technologies that drive today's digital world.

www.ingramcontent.com/pod-product-compliance
Lightning Source LLC
LaVergne TN
LVHW070855210926
848482LV00016B/940

* 9 7 9 8 2 9 5 6 2 3 5 9 2 *